THE LIFE OF
KNOWLES SHAW
THE
Singing Evangelist

by
William Baxter

Charleston, AR:
COBB PUBLISHING
2017

The Life of Knowles Shaw, the Singing Evangelist (updated and corrected edition) is copyright © Bradley S. Cobb, 2017. All rights reserved. Any republishing (i.e., in print) of this edition is a violation of US copyright laws, and is also a sin.

We have made this edition available as a free download in the Jimmie Beller Memorial eLibrary, at TheCobbSix.com. Feel free to download it there and share it with your friends.

Published in the United States of America by:

Cobb Publishing
704 E. Main St.
Charleston, AR 72933
(479) 747-8372
CobbPublishing@gmail.com
TheCobbSix.com
CobbPbulishing.com

ISBN: 978-1-947622-02-9

Publisher's Preface

If this book doesn't encourage you to be more active and energetic in showing your Christianity, then you need to have a serious reevaluation of your spiritual life.

Knowles Shaw was a hard-working, dedicated evangelist, who showed the way of truth to thousands throughout his life. His name is all but forgotten by most in the church today (except for the history buffs), but still we sing songs that he wrote ("Bringing in the Sheaves") or put music to ("We Saw Thee Not"). So he still has some influence, whether we realized it or not.

This book was originally written in 1879 by William Baxter. This edition differs from the original only slightly—spelling has been updated to modern usage, any Bible references have been changed to the current format (i.e., instead of "iii. 16" it would be "3:16"), any typos have been corrected, and the entire book has undergone a facelift, with a change in page size, font size, etc. In other words, we've kept the book the way it was, but made it look a whole lot nicer.

We hope you find this book as uplifting as we did.

Bradley S. Cobb
July, 2017

Author's Preface

This book is not the outgrowth of the author's mind, but the record of a life which was, in many respects, a very remarkable one. The material for the book consisted of the manuscripts of the deceased, reports of his work as found in various journals, both secular and religious, and the personal recollections of those who knew and loved him. The writer's work has been mainly that of collecting and arranging the material from the sources above mentioned. To one and all who have aided in the work, I tender my hearty thanks, and feel that it will be a pleasure for them to know that they have helped to place in a permanent form an account of the life and labors of one so worthy of being remembered.

That the hearts of the readers may be stirred, as mine has been while writing this brief story of an earnest, unselfish, and useful life, is the wish of the

Author.

Table of Contents

Chapter One 1

Birth and Parentage—Removal to Indiana—State of Society— A Disaster—Death of his Father—His Legacy—A Famous Fiddler—Jack of all Trades—Sowing Wild Oats.

Chapter Two 8

Sudden Change—Scene in a Ball-Room—Mental Conflict— Battle with the Devil—His Baptism—Thirst for Knowledge—Marriage—Decides to be a Preacher

Chapter Three 14

Student and Teacher—Preacher and Temperance Lecturer— Success in the Ministry—Method of Working—Analysis of his Character—Sketch by T.W. Caskey.

Chapter Four 20

Remarkable Meetings—Lebanon, Ohio—Wellsburg, West Virginia, and Other Places—Labors in 1875-76

Chapter Five 36

His Love for the Lost—Blue Dick—Labors in the Murphy Movement—Singing "Lambs of the Upper Fold" at a Childs Funeral.

Chapter Six 43

Meeting at St. Louis—Great Interest—Reports of the Press—Results.

Chapter Seven 59

Anecdotes—A Change of Heart Wanted—Scoffer Silenced— Danger of Immersion—Slanderer Reproved— Universalists Answered—Convention Quieted—Humorous Answers.

Chapter Eight 65
Sketches of Several Sermons—"It is I; be not Afraid"—Pearl of Great Price — Deceitfulness of Sin — Smooth Things—Good Works—Triumphs of the Gospel.

Chapter Nine 75
Domestic Life—Death of His Daughter—Her Dying Words—His Dream—Musical Talent—Musical Publications—Estimate of His Musical Powers—"Bringing in the Sheaves."

Chapter Ten 82
Moody and Shaw Compared and Contrasted— Extracts from the Sermons of Both—Moody's Ticket and Shaw's.

Chapter Eleven 90
Need of Mental Photograph—A Specimen Sermon—How Readest Thou?— What Lack I Yet?

Chapter Twelve 98
Not a Eulogy, but a Life—Pen Portrait by David Walk— Meeting at Memphis—Notices by the Memphis Press.

Chapter Thirteen 109
The Editor of the Christian Preacher on Shaw's Method and Manner—Elder Caskey's Review of Wilmeth, and Opinion of Shaw—The Editor's Rejoinder.

Chapter Fourteen 116
Extent and Variety of His Labors—Extracts from Diary for 1877— Last Day at Home.

Chapter Fifteen 125
Brother Shaw's Last Meeting—His Last Day—An Account of the Wreck.

Chapter Sixteen 135
Funeral Services at Dallas—Closing Services, and Burial at Rushville, Indiana.

Chapter Seventeen 144
Difference Between Our Judgments Concerning the Living and the Dead—Memorial Service at Columbus, Mississippi.

Chapter Eighteen 160
A Sad Scene—Strange Coincidence—Lines by G.W. Archer—Tribute of Affection—Memorial Service at Jackson, Mississippi—In Memoriam.

Chapter Nineteen 171
Poem—What the "Christian" and "Standard" Said—Challen's Last Song—Farewell.

Chapter One

Birth and Parentage—Removal to Indiana—State of Society— A Disaster—Death of his Father— His Legacy—A Famous Fiddler—Jack of all Trades—Sowing Wild Oats.

Knowles Shaw was born in Butler County, Ohio, on the 13th of October, 1834. His father, Albin Shaw, and mother, whose maiden name was Huldah Griffin, were of Scotch descent. A few weeks after the birth of Knowles, their first child, they removed to Rush County, Indiana. That portion of the State was at that time a new settlement; indeed the whole State was then regarded as being "out West." The population was a poor but hardy class of people, but, as the sequel has proved, possessing the elements necessary for growth and prosperity. The extent of this growth since the time of which we write is indeed marvelous; from a forest it has become a fruitful field; from a new country, destitute of nearly all the comforts and blessings of civilized life, it has become, within the memory of those yet living, dotted over with large towns and cities, alive with busy trade and the hum of manufactories, while its railways, like the arms of a giant, gather the products of all the lands between the oceans. Its advancement in mental and moral culture has kept pace with its material prosperity; the change from the almost unbroken forest to the cultivated farm has not been greater than that from the scanty, as well as rude facilities for instruction to those of every grade now so abundant, from the everywhere present common school to the university, rich in all the appliances of scientific and classic learning.

The parents of the subject of our story belonged to the humble hard-working class, which form the chief element of all new settlements, and his early days were spent amid the hardships and privations inseparable from a pioneer life. What he was in after life was not on account of any favorable surroundings in his earlier years, for the early settlers in this then new country had too hard a struggle in subduing the forest and gaining a scanty subsistence to pay much attention to either moral or intellectual culture. The means and helps to such improvements, as in all new localities, were either wanting or of the rudest description, nor were the schoolmasters and preachers of the time wholly unsuited to the somewhat unsightly buildings in which the elements of learning and religion were taught. During the summer and fall, religious meetings were often held under the shade of the beeches, or in a grove of tall shapely sugar-trees, the hearers finding natural seats on fallen trees, or on the green sward— usually, however, the rude log building; with its puncheon floor, clapboard roof, openings for windows, admitting at the same time light and air, and benches with unsteady legs and without backs; which during the portions of the year that could not be profitably employed in outdoor labor was used as a school-house, served as a church as often as some John the Baptist of a brighter dispensation not far distant was found to call the people to repentance or point them to a land, which to all seemed a better land because it was a land of rest.

In bad weather the leaky roof and open crannies, which permitted the cold blast to enter too freely, was a great cause of discomfort, and as stoves had not come into general use, their place was sometimes supplied by huge iron sugar-kettles, in which charcoal fires were kept burning, making it more than warm enough for those who sat near them, while those more remote were often pinched with cold. Both heat and cold, however, were endured without complaint, for preaching was uncommon enough to be a luxury, no matter how cold or hot the house might be; and there are those yet who go back in fond memory to those days, and think that heaven seemed nearer then, with only a roof that could not keep out the rain, than now, with frescoed ceilings, cushioned seats, light softened by stained glass, spire pointing heavenward, and the bell calling all to the house of prayer.

It was in this very region that Edward Eggleston laid the scene and found much of his material for the "Hoosier Schoolmaster," and "The End of the World"—novels and romances we call them—but many of the scenes are drawn from real life in Southeastern Indiana, less than forty years ago. The writer of these pages spent several days at a Millerite camp-meeting in that region in the summer of 1843, when the "End of the World," the second coming of Christ, was looked for daily, nay hourly, and heard from the lips of those who were waiting and wishing for the coming of the Son of

Man in the clouds of heaven, the wonderful dreams they had, and the strange portents written on the face of the midnight sky, which assured them beyond all doubt that the day of the Lord was at hand. The stirring exhortations and the sweet songs, which woke the forest echoes ever and anon during the night-watches, and which welcomed each dawn which might be the dawn of the last day of time, are still fresh in my memory, and the glad hopes of those who had given up all earthly interests in full assurance that the time was at hand, and the fears of those not fully convinced and wholly unprepared for such an event, made an impression on my mind of which none but those who mingled in those scenes can form the slightest conception.

It was not far from this locality that young Shaw, then a boy of some nine or ten years of age, was then living. His lot in life, as already intimated, was a lowly one: toil and privation came as soon as he was able to endure the one and feel the other. Nothing in his horizon seemed hopeful, nothing to indicate that he would be known beyond the very narrow circle in which he moved. A heart here and there among companions as humble as himself he might bind to his own in friendship or love, but beyond this nothing but a toiler and plodder, who would soon leave as little trace of himself in the great world around as the traveler whose footprints on the sea-shore are effaced by the first returning tide. In the meantime two other children, a boy and girl, had been added to the family, making greater the demands upon the labors of the father, which were freely given—for children are even more welcome in the cottage of the poor than the abode of wealth and luxury—in the former case being the greatest and almost only joy.

Albin Shaw loved his children, and made every effort in an honorable way to secure for them such advantages as would fit them for usefulness in after life, or to leave them and their mother a competency in the event of his being early called away. To this end he labored with his hands, as farmer and tanner, traded in cattle at one time, and finally engaged in selling goods in a small village in Rush County. He would sometimes collect the three children around him and prognosticate their future by examining their heads. That of his oldest son was a puzzle to him: his conclusion was that he would make a terrible bad man or a very good one; that whatever he did he would do with all his might,

Knowles, though but a child, was always busy, and one of his early inventions came near proving a serious disaster. Like most boys he was fond of firearms; he made a wooden gun and loaded it, but all his efforts to make it go off were in vain. As a last resort he dropped a coal of fire into the muzzle, which produced the desired effect sooner than he expected, and his face was severely burned. Smarting with pain he got a coarse towel and rubbed off the blistered skin, to escape, as he afterward explained, being powder-marked. It is needless to say that this was an end to experiments in that direction.

But a sad and unlooked for calamity was at hand. The father, the bread-winner of the family, was taken sick, soon became worse, and one day feeling that the end was near, had Knowles called to his bedside to give him his parting words. They were few and brief—little more than, "My son, be good to your mother," and, "Prepare to meet your God." His last gift was a violin, which had often been a solace to him in his life of toil, and soon after the weary toiler closed his eyes on what had been a world of toil and care to open them on earth no more.

This event to the family was a great calamity, making their hard lot harder still, and brought upon young Shaw, then about twelve years of age, cares and responsibilities unknown before. Boy as he was, he strove to make his mother's burden lighter, and labored to the full extent of his ability to aid her in raising her dependent family. He grew to be a stout, hearty youth, able when but a boy in years to do a man's work; and this he did not only without complaint, but cheerfully, showing that the dying father's words, "Be good to your mother," had not been forgotten. Nor did he forget his father's legacy, the old violin. From infancy music had been a passion; and now all his spare moments, when the toils of the day were over, were devoted to his father's gift, and he soon was able to play upon it with the ease and skill known only to a born musician. A talent like this could not be kept secret. The neighbors would often drop in to see the widow Shaw, but never left until Knowles had been called on for a tune—one only paved the way for another, and the evening would wear into night before the listeners were aware how the hours had sped by. It soon came to pass that he was invited to play at other places than at home; and in a short time no social gathering or merry-making of any kind was complete unless enlivened by the merry strains of his violin.

But under all this there lurked a great danger; and when the circumstances are known there is little cause for wonder that he fell into the snare. One of the greatest evils of the times of which we write was intemperance. At all gatherings in a new settlement, no matter what the object might be, whisky seemed a necessity. A political gathering without this stimulant to patriotism was unknown; the candidate for office who was not willing to treat those whose votes he sought was very likely to obtain but few on election day, while he who furnished a good supply of the *ardent* did not lack a goodly number of ardent supporters. The harvest could not be gathered without liquor; a house or barn-raising, or corn-husking, generally ended in a drunken revel. At weddings and all merry-makings liquor was used without stint, and it was not even banished from funerals, for it seemed to possess the power of exciting mirth and assuaging the bitterness of grief. Large religious meetings were not entirely free from its presence, and if a preacher indulged in a little, he was thought none the less devout on that account. Whisky was indispensable at the meeting of friends, and a little was also deemed necessary at parting, and to refuse the proffered glass was a species of rudeness almost unheard of.

Brought up amid such surroundings it is not to be wondered at that young Shaw, who was of a social, lively and excitable temperament, should soon acquire a taste for strong drink. He was the life of every social gathering, a favorite especially with the young, his musical skill the admiration of the whole settlement, and it is not to be wondered at that he was often the soul of the revel and the gayest of the gay. Hundreds of young people in those days danced to his music; every year witnessed an increase of his skill, and with it was an increased demand for his presence and services. He sang a good song, had quite a vein of mimicry, and, though rude and unpolished, he seemed less so from his constant mingling in society than many of his rude companions, and, it must be added, came near being drawn into the vortex of dissipation beyond the power of successful resistance. In addition to what we have said above, there was another feature in the course he was pursuing that had a great tendency to keep and confirm him in it. His musical talent had become a source of profit. At every gathering where his services were in demand a sum of money, sometimes quite a handsome one, was the reward of his skill. This money he never wasted. He remembered well the injunction of his dying father: "Be good to your mother;" and into her hands went nearly all his gains. Even up to this period, when he was rapidly changing from boyhood to manhood, he seems to have thought of no higher career than that into which he had insensibly drifted. No one dreamed of him being very much different from what he was, and he had no higher ambition than that of being a good fellow and the best fiddler in the settlement.

Though content with this he had abilities in other directions; none, however, so marked, or in such demand as his talent for music. In other respects many of his companions were his equals, but in music he bore away the palm. His father, as we have seen, was merchant, stock-dealer, tanner, farmer, and also possessed of some musical taste and skill. In this ability to turn his hand to almost anything his son not only resembled, but greatly excelled him. He learned to make shoes in a single week, made grain-cradles for the neighbors, was a carpenter, plasterer, and on one occasion greatly astonished a watchmaker from whom he obtained permission to use his tools, by taking his watch to pieces, cleaning it, and putting it together again in good order, as if cleaning a watch were an everyday affair with him. He knew so many things from the habit of close observation that he had cultivated, that one of the neighbors quaintly expressed the general sentiment in regard to him by saying that "Knowles Shaw's head was like a tar-bucket, for everything that touched it stuck to it."

After he grew older he spent a short time as a clerk in a store, taught school several terms, and having at one time fallen in with a teacher who professed to be able to give instructions in Greek and Latin, he became a pupil, and in one month learned all his teacher knew. Whether this was due to the aptness of the pupil, or to the meager attainments of the teacher, tradition does not inform us. But we are anticipating the order of events, and must resume the thread of our narrative.

He was now nearly eighteen years of age, a man in size, tall, angular, somewhat awkward, but kind-hearted, good-tempered, and industrious, which rendered him a general favorite.

As far as book-learning was concerned, he was extremely deficient. The few facilities for improvement that might have been used he was obliged to neglect, in order to meet the demands made upon him by the family, which regarded him as their chief dependence. To labor for them seemed a pleasure, as well as a duty, and the self-denial he had to practice in order to provide for them was cheerfully endured.

It will not surprise the reader, in view of what has been said in regard to the company he kept and the habits he had learned, that he did not seem to be religiously inclined. His position to Christianity, however, was rather that of neglect and indifference than of dislike and opposition. The gay and thoughtless were his companions. Like himself, many of them were "sowing their wild oats," without stopping to ask the question, What shall the harvest be? And nothing doubtless, at this period, would have seemed more improbable to him and all who knew him than that he should become a Christian, and also a preacher of that faith to others.

Previous to this time the movement called the Reformation, but more generally known as "Campbellism," had made considerable progress in Rush County, being advocated with great zeal and ability by several preachers whose names have long been household words, not only in that locality but all over the State and throughout the West—such as Elder Benjamin Franklin, H.R. Pritchard, B.K. Smith, and George Campbell. Several churches had been organized, and, among others, one known as the Flat Rock congregation, in the neighborhood where young Shaw was living.

The views of the new religious party of course had given rise to much discussion, and the controversial discourses of the ministers of other bodies, who disputed its claims, and those of that body, in turn in defense, gave more than usual interest to the preaching of that period, especially when a man of more than ordinary ability from either party was to hold forth. On such occasions large crowds were wont to assemble, and among them the young fiddler, not from any special interest, perhaps, in the subject under discussion, but because everybody was there.

Chapter Two

Sudden Change—Scene in a Ball-Room—Mental Conflict— Battle with the Devil—His Baptism— Thirst for Knowledge—Marriage—Decides to be a Preacher.

But a nature like his was not to run wild and to waste; a nobler career than that of ministering to the pleasures of the thoughtless and mirth-loving was soon to open before him; instead of being the leader in every scene of gaiety and folly, he was soon to enter upon a life of lofty purpose and toil, and to turn the feet of thousands into the way of righteousness and peace.

This great change in the current of his thoughts and life was sudden, and had a strange beginning. One night he was playing the violin for a large company of dancers, and in that most unlikely of all places for serious thought, there came into his mind the dying advice of his father, in the impressive words of the prophet: "Prepare to meet thy God." They came unbidden; they forced themselves upon him with a power that he could not resist; they seemed to him not only a voice from the grave but a message from heaven. Still the dance went on; but the gayer the crowd became, the sadder grew the heart of the player, whose mirthful strains were at such variance with the solemn thoughts with which his mind was occupied.

A young lady observing the sadness of his look, and the abstraction of his manner, approached him and said: "Knowly, what is the matter?" He told without reserve the state of his mind; and it was with strange feelings that she resumed her place through the set, to music which she knew mocked the feelings of the sad-hearted player. The dance ceased; another set was formed, and all were waiting for the music to begin. To the astonishment of all, Shaw, in response to the call to "strike up," said he could not play anymore. A dozen voices called on him to begin, when he gravely walked out into the middle of the floor and told all that had been passing through his mind; told of his father's dying words, neglected till then, and expressed his determination never to play for another dance. He expressed regret for his past course of life; that it was not such as it should have been; that it might do if this life were all; but in view of the life to come, he must pursue another course. He then asked the company, about forty in all, to promise that they would throw no hindrance in the way of his attempt to lead a new life. His sadness, manliness, and earnestness reached their hearts. They gave the promise he asked; and to their honor be it said, they not only kept it, but some of them even gave him help and encouragement to keep the resolve which under such strange surroundings he had made. This proved to be no passing fancy; it was the turning point in his life; and to the life which he had been leading he never from that hour longingly looked back.

It must be remembered that this was the act of a somewhat rough and uneducated country boy, but only the nobler and more remarkable on that account. It displayed a moral courage, heroic as well as rare, and showed the awakening of a great soul to the solemn duties and responsibilities of life.

In a mood far different from his usual one on leaving such scenes of festivity, he reached his home that night, and found his mother sitting up for him. But his manner was greatly changed; instead of a lively description of the great dancing party, and imitations of the various characters there, which his talent for mimicry often led him to indulge in, he was silent and thoughtful. He asked for a bowl of bread and milk, and when he had eaten asked for a blanket, and wrapped in this he passed the night on the floor. For several days he ate nothing but a little bread and milk, and spent the nights on the floor, wrapped in his blanket. During this time he seldom closed his eyes, and was evidently passing through a severe mental conflict. To his mother's frequent entreaties to tell her his trouble, he made reply that he was having a battle with the devil.

All the difficulties of the course he had entered upon came vividly before him; the possibility of the family suffering for lack of the help his violin had enabled him to afford them; the difficulty of providing for them by manual labor; the power of appetite to which he had yielded; the associations which he had formed which must be broken, made those sleepless nights seem long and terrible. Any thought of yielding he regarded as the whispering of the devil; he struggled on and was victorious.

He now began to attend the services at the Flat Rock Church

with a feeling and purpose far different from that which had taken him there before; the clear scriptural views presented were like light from heaven to one who had long walked in darkness; and after a sermon from Gabriel McDuffie, and an exhortation by Elder George Campbell, he publicly confessed his faith in Jesus Christ, and was immersed by George Thomas, the elder of the church, on the 13th of September, 1852.

What a treasure now would be a full report of the doings of that bright autumn day; the discourse of "Uncle Gabriel," as the preacher was affectionately called; the exhortation of George Campbell, a Boanerges in zeal, and rising, as many still remember, when calling sinners to repentance, to the highest degree of tender and pathetic entreaty; the company gathered on the banks of the stream; the words of prayer at the administration of the solemn rite; the sweet song at the close, and the serene joy of the young convert, in the assurance that he was Christ's, and that Christ was his. All this must be left to the imagination. But one thing is certain: that there would have been even a deeper feeling and an intenser joy could the godly men who took part in the doings of that day have foreseen the multitudes the young convert should bring to the Master's feet. As it was, to young Shaw it was a day never to be forgotten. From that hour, life had to him a new meaning; it was no longer to be a mere struggle for the bread that perishes, but an endeavor for a better life beyond the present—a race in which an immortal crown might be won.

Many predicted that he would soon be as careless and jolly as ever; and when they observed the attention paid him by Uncle Gabriel McDuffie, under whose ministry he had been converted, and who strove to help and encourage him all in his power, they said, with a sneering smile: "The old man is wasting his time on Shaw; he'll soon be back in the ball-room, fiddling as lively as ever." This came to Shaw's ears, and he said that he hoped to prove himself worthy of the old brother's attention and care; he conducted himself toward him as a son in the gospel, and it cheered the old man's heart to find that the seed he had sown was not in vain.

He now felt more painfully than ever his lack of education, and at once set about to remedy that defect. In consequence of being compelled to labor constantly to supply the needs of those who were dependent upon him, his progress was slow; still he contrived to gather and retain much useful knowledge. He had an excellent memory, a quick and lively fancy, some readiness of expression; and these all combined had the effect of making him seem better informed than many who had enjoyed far superior advantages, but who could not use as freely as he the stores which they possessed. It must not be inferred from the above that he had attained to any great degree of scholarship. Such was not the case. In even elementary training he was extremely deficient; but he made the best possible use of what he heard and read, and thus laid up a magazine of facts which he was able to turn to a good account in after years.

His thirst for knowledge increased with every acquisition; and while he had not the least idea at that time of entering public life, he was unconsciously preparing himself for such a work as that to which he afterward was providentially called. He was a faithful and consistent member of the church all this time, growing stronger every day, and highly esteemed by his fellow-members.

Over two years of such a life as we have described passed away, and we find him working as a farm hand for one of the neighbors, Mr. George R. Finley, for whose daughter Martha he in process of time conceived a high regard. This feeling was mutual, and ripened into something more than esteem; and it was soon the old story, that has been repeated over and over again. They became more than all besides to each other, and they were married on the 11th of January, 1855. He was at this time only a few months over twenty years of age, poor in this world's goods, but hopeful and buoyant in spirit. With a stout heart and strong hands, he saw no reason why life should not be a success.

Nearly four years of his married life passed, one of which was spent in Missouri, with little to mark it beyond what is common to an industrious, hardworking man. Each day brought its toil, and at the same time the simple home-born joys, which are the dearest heritage of the poor. During these years the young couple were blessed with two children, Georgie Anna, born on the 3rd of June, 1856, and Mary Elizabeth, born on the 31st of October, 1858. All this time Knowles was faithful in the discharge of his religious duties; would now and then take some humble part in the sacred services, but gave no special promise of future usefulness beyond that of a humble, godly life. On one occasion, at a grove meeting, he was called on to say something. He rose and said: "Brethren and sisters, I have not very much to say; but I am thankful to the Lord for the mercy he has shown me. When I first joined the church I thought that was all I had to do; but one day Squire Layton said to me: 'Shaw, if you were out of corn, and some kind, good man, would say, "Come to my crib and get all the corn you want, and I will charge you nothing for it," would you take the corn and go away without thanking him?' I replied, 'No, sir.' 'Then,' added he, 'when the Lord gives you the hope of everlasting life, will you not thank him?' I said, 'Yes.' And I do thank him from the depths of my heart."

As already intimated, he had made some efforts at self-improvement, and not wholly in vain; but his knowledge was fragmentary, and as yet he was almost entirely without that training of the mind which alone deserves the name of education.

On the third Lord's Day of October, 1858, from some cause or other, he was called on to talk to the people who had gathered for worship. He made the attempt with some diffidence and confusion at first; but gradually gaining his self-possession, he made a brief address, marked by such good sense, and delivered with such unaffected earnestness, that his hearers were satisfied that they had before them one possessed of the elements of a successful preacher. As a trial sermon before an assemblage of ministers, it would doubtless have been regarded as greatly lacking in most of the elements of a popular address; but his hearers judged by their hearts, by what they felt, and the decision rendered by nearly all was that Knowles Shaw would make a preacher. No one was more surprised at the effect of the discourse than the speaker himself. In his deep regard and warm admiration for the men upon whose ministry he had attended with such profit and pleasure, he had not thought it possible that he could ever become such an instrument of good to his fellows as they. The ice, however, was fairly broken; many were convinced that he possessed the elements of great usefulness. Frequent opportunities were afforded for the exercise of his newly-found talent, and each exercise of it served to confirm the first impression he had made.

He was now twenty-four years of age, with less confidence in his natural abilities for public life and usefulness than most of those who were advising him to that course, and with a far deeper consciousness of his defective, nay, almost utter lack of education.

This was one of the great turning points in his life, and what was duty, was pondered over with an intensity not inferior to that which marked the period described in the preceding portion of the chapter, when, during the watches of many a sleepless night, he struggled against Satan and gained a victory.

That one in such a lowly condition in life, and so little enlightened in point of learning, should feel so deeply may appear strange; but it must not be forgotten that he was both poet and musician, and though his powers as such had not been developed to any great extent at this time, he had even then the musician's sensitive nature and the poet's heart. There was slumbering in his breast at that time a power to move men which no man among the hundreds of thousands among his brethren ever possessed to the same degree—a power possessed by few in this generation—and it was this that made a mental struggle greater with him than with other men. Prayer, and deep, earnest reflection, marked these days. The advice of trusted friends, especially that of Uncle Gabriel, was carefully weighed; and the result was a decision to devote his days to the great work of preaching the gospel of Jesus Christ.

Chapter Three

Student and Teacher—Preacher and Temperance Lecturer— Success in the Ministry—Method of Working—Analysis of his Character— Sketch by T.W. Caskey.

His true vocation was found at last, and to it he felt all his powers must be made tributary; and his future life showed an entire consecration to his work. His education at this time was little more than begun, and for some time he was teacher and pupil— teaching what he knew in the district school, and at the same time learning as he could, what was most important for him to know in regard to the life work on which he had entered.

One of his pupils at that time, but now a lawyer in Rush County, says, "the district in which Shaw taught had rather a bad name, the boys generally managing the school instead of the teacher. The first day of the term we were all on hand, wondering how he would suit, and from what we had heard of him rather inclined to think that our rule would continue. Our teacher was a very tall man, three or four inches over six feet, rather slender, with large hands and feet—able, from all appearance, to enforce whatever rules he might prescribe. He had an agreeable voice, and quite a pleasant expression of countenance; and the first impression was a favorable one. He called the school to order, and gave us his rules; indeed, he had but one, which he announced somewhat as follows: 'Boys, I expect you to do as I do; what I do and say you are at liberty to do and say; if I lie, you can lie; if I swear, you can swear; if I fight, you can fight; but if you do any of these things and I don't, you will get a whipping.' No one was whipped that term. There was crying done at the close of the term by nearly all of us, but it was because we had to part with our teacher, whom we had soon come to regard as our best friend. When there was any work to be done about the school-house or yard he was always first to begin, and then say, 'Come on' to the boys, who never refused to follow his example. We all got to like him, and when he preached we were sure to be present. We also got him to make temperance addresses, and we all did our part to make such meetings a success. I remember well when he was to make his first temperance speech, that an old toper who was there was talking very hard about Shaw before he came, on account of his views on temperance; but when he came the old man went in to hear him, and before the lecture was over he was crying like a child, and said he had never seen the subject in that light before."

All this time he was preaching, whenever and wherever he found an opportunity. His improvement was very marked. He began to receive invitations to preach at various places in the county, and when scarcely a year had passed after he entered fully upon his work, he was regarded as a useful man, and one who gave great promise of increased usefulness in the future. His musical talent, too, now began to attract far more attention than when his skill on the violin was the admiration of all the pleasure-loving people for miles around; even more than by his preaching, were multitudes moved and melted by his songs; and soon he was widely known as the "Singing Evangelist."

He was now fairly launched upon his wonderful career, which brought so much toil to him, and so much blessedness to those for whom his labor was given. Conversions began to attend his labors, and this only stimulated him to greater effort. God, he felt, was thus owning his work in the salvation of his fellow-men.

The first record we can find of his success is in the *Millennial Harbinger* for 1861, only about two years after he began to preach. It is as follows:

> *Brother Knowles Shaw, a young evangelist, writing from Rushville, Indiana, says: "At all my meetings this year some sixty persons have enlisted under the banner of Christ."*

Under date of August 28th, of the same year, we hear from him again in these terms:

> *At our meeting in Hamilton County there were three additions by confession and immersion. Brother Van Winkle was with us during the meeting. At a meeting at New Hope, of ten days' continuance, there were fifty-one additions—forty-three by confession and baptism. Brother H.R. Pritchard was with us a part of the time. We also held a meeting in Madison County, where there were seventeen*

> *additions. And during our last visit to the brethren at Little Flat Rock there were four additions. We have determined to preach the gospel, the whole gospel, and nothing but the gospel, to the best of our ability.*

His life had always been one of great activity. It was not less so now, but in an entire different direction. He knew nothing of the usual routine of a preacher's life, either in his preparation for his work or the actual performance of it. Of theology he knew nothing, only as he had heard it from the pulpits of the various religious parties, and he had no narrow creed of his own to cramp and fetter his powers. Instead of living in a library, with books only for his companions, and bringing before the people once or twice a week the results of his reading and study, he came before them with a message drawn from the one Book, and suited to the wants of men in all the various conditions in which they are found. He was the farthest possible remove from the conventional preacher in almost every particular—in dress, manners, habits, and intercourse with men; and the reader will fail utterly in his conception of him if he thinks of him as an average modern preacher, differing in only a few unimportant particulars from all the rest of his class. He lived among the people whom he taught and strove to save, as one of them; his visits were not of a solemn and formal character; he sought them in the shop, the forest, the field; a street conversation was often the occasion of impressing serious reflections on the minds of those he met. Instead of delaying the work of those he called upon, he would take hold and help while he talked, and thus release them from anything like constraint; learn all their wants, doubts, troubles, and also enter into their joys, and leave them better far for the call and with minds made up, even without an invitation, to hear him preach the next Sunday without fail. He had a song for the children of the families that he dropped in to see, and cheered the parents, while apparently seeking to please the children. If the clock was out of order, a few touches from his hand would often set it right; if the sewing-machine would not work it was soon in smooth running order, and the good wife thought no less of the preacher who was so handy, and not at all stuck up, but just like other folks.

Few men could get better acquainted in a strange place sooner than he. During one of his meetings he would be going nearly all the time, from morning till night, going into nearly every place of business, and getting acquainted with everybody. If a death took place he needed no invitation to attend the funeral, and sometimes gave consolation, which was all the sweeter to the sorrowing from the fact that it was the offering of a stranger. Once when in a strange city he wandered out to the graveyard. While there a young child was brought for burial; the parents were not members of any church; he joined the sad company, talked a little at the grave, sang one of his tender songs, and made such an impression on the mourning ones that they came to hear him preach that same evening.

In this way he made himself acquainted with human life in all its phases, and by mingling freely with society during the week, he knew how to meet their various wants when he met them on Sunday at the house of God. His chief studies were the Bible and human nature, and the great secret of his power over men consisted in first learning their precise needs, and then meeting those needs with what the word of God furnished. This made his sermons often lack in unity; but if varied they were not more so than the circumstances of his hearers, and when the greatest number of those was reached his end was accomplished.

He was fertile in illustration; his knowledge of men and things gave him a rich store of striking similes and figures. He drew largely, also, from his own experience, and, though neither learned nor profound, he seldom failed in one way or other to reach every one of his hearers. But, above all, he was deeply in earnest; all who came in contact with him realized that. He needed not the inspiration of a crowd to call forth his powers; if he had but few, or, as on a few occasions, but one or two, he seemed to realize the value of the soul, and talked earnestly and tenderly, as did the Master to a few disciples, or to the woman at the well. He did not seem to have the wish, even if he had the power, to make fine speeches; he spoke more for effect, to tell the sick of a cure, to point out the way to the lost.

One or two carefully-prepared sermons per week did not come up to his ideal; the souls of men were always in danger; to save them he felt that he must be always at work. A discourse for every day in the week even was not deemed enough; three per day were not uncommon, and sometimes four. Besides this, he labored much from house to house, doing good as he had opportunity—when opportunity seemed lacking he made one. His powers were so varied that during the progress of a meeting he reached the case of all the classes who came to hear him. One of our most eminent preachers in the South, Elder Caskey, a fine judge of human nature, and who met Shaw when in the height of his usefulness and made him his study, observed this peculiarity to which we have called attention, and to it attributed much of his success. He says:

> *He had his peculiar style of saying things and doing things; he conformed to no standard, either of oratory or action; as a logician he was not profound; as a word-painter I have heard him excelled; as for pathos, I have heard others who were his superiors in that respect. I am under the impression that his power was owing to a combination of these three elements, that, singly or combined, make up the greatness of all eminent speakers. This combination he possessed in a greater degree than any speaker I have ever heard. The reason, perhaps, why he excelled in neither was the absence, to some extent, of what phrenological science calls continuity of thought. When he played the logician, which he could do, it was sharp, cogent, incisive, but always short, never exhaustive. He seemed not to have the power to drive his mental machinery along the track for any considerable length of time, or chose not to do it; his transitions from logic to rhetoric, from reasoning to description, from the serious to the humorous, from tragedy to comedy, were sudden and frequent; consequently there was often a mingling of smiles and tears among the impressible of those who heard him. Versatility was a leading element of his nature. As a musician he had few equals; his power of imitation was wonderful; he could imitate the joyous, strong-faithed Christian, by gestures, looks and words, until you could almost see the sparkle of his eye, the flush on his face, the happy smile on his lips, and hear his glad shout ringing in your ear; then suddenly he would put on a long face, the woe-begone look, the drooping form, and heave the burdened sigh of some poor, doubting, halting, and*

fearing, John Bunyan- made-Christian, on his way to the Castle of Giant Despair.

This versatility, so well sketched above, was characteristic of him in the beginning of his evangelical labors, as well as at the period when the above picture was drawn—not under as perfect control, perhaps, at first, as in after years, but, nevertheless, the great and marked peculiarity of the man. With this key to his character we can understand fully why it was that success and usefulness were attained so early. What others reached, in even a small degree, after years of study and patient toil, he reached in a high degree without their advantages, in a much briefer period. In 1860 his work was only fairly begun, but in the ten years following he held more successful meetings than any man in our ranks. Within four or five years from the beginning of his public labors he attracted much attention, and met with great success; and at that early day, when only about thirty years of age, held meetings not inferior in interest and results to those with which we have become so familiar in the later years of his life. He was a growing, successful preacher from the beginning; he never slackened his efforts, but worked while it was called today.

Among his earlier meetings, one held at Tipton, Indiana, is especially worthy of note. This was in May and June, 1864. It was held in the Courthouse, and was attended by great throngs of people.

The excitement is compared, by one who was present, to that of a heated political campaign—the people coming from far and near, and resulting in one hundred and thirty-two additions to the church. Among them was a youth only thirteen years of age—at this writing twenty-eight years of age, who has been preaching the gospel for years, and has persuaded hundreds to turn from the evil of their ways. In connection with Brother Pritchard, he had even greater success in a meeting at Jonesville, Indiana, in 1865. This brings us to the most active period of his life, his work fully entered upon, his purposes formed to spend, and be spent, in the work to which he was providentially called. The future chapters will contain the progress of that work, which was one of battles which were victories.

Chapter Four

Remarkable Meetings—Lebanon, Ohio—Wellsburg, West Virginia, and Other Places—Labors in 1875-76

The record of his meetings, and the matters of interest connected with them, would, fill a volume, and, while it would be impossible to give all, yet it would be a serious defect to omit a notice of some of his most successful ones. We give a list of twenty of them, and the number added at each.

Lebanon, Ohio	252
Buchanan, Michigan	226
St. Louis, Missouri	150
Harrison, Ohio	144
Jonesville, Indiana	138
Jeffersonville, Indiana	118
Wellsburg, West Virginia	120
Dallas, Texas	112
Charlestown, Indiana	112
Covington, Kentucky	105
Centerville, Iowa	103
Quincy, Illinois	87
Canton, Missouri	78
Sterling, Illinois	79
Clarksville, Tennessee	67
Hamilton, Ohio	122
Waynesville, Ohio	61
Rushville, Indiana	56
Little Flat Rock, Indiana	56
Warsaw, Indiana	50
Total	**2236**

It must be remembered, however, that these are but a few out of a multitude. Only a few months before his death he stated that he had not been out of a protracted meeting for two weeks in succession for thirteen years. With regard to the first place on the foregoing list, he wrote, one year after the organization of the church, as follows:

THE CHURCH IN LEBANON.

LEBANON, OHIO, *February 8, 1869.*

Brother Errett:—This day, one year ago, the Church of Christ was organized here with fourteen members.

The meeting had commenced January 8, 1868, in Washington Hall. I knew of but two brethren and their wives here before coming to hold the meeting; found a few others after my arrival. Some of the members in the organization were new converts. Many were the prophecies of failure as this little band stood up and gave each other the hand of fellowship and Christian love, pledging to each other their unfaltering friendship and love in Christ, to stand by each other in persecution, trial, or prosperity, as it might best please our kind heavenly Father.

The tear-dimmed eyes of that little company spoke eloquently to the crowd assembled, mainly from curiosity, of their sincerity and devotion to the cause of truth.

The question, 'Does the church still live?' is one often asked. I will briefly answer.

Yes, thank God, it lives; and not only lives, but prospers. 'Tis pleasant to look back over the year past and see the steps by which this advance has been made.

We have gained every inch of ground by the severest contests. We can adopt the language of the old hymn: 'We have fought our way through.' We hope to be able to adopt the rest after awhile. The aggregate number of members enlisted during the year is nearly two hundred and ninety. Of these twelve have been withdrawn from, two or three of whom have returned; some have removed to other parts, taking letters; some have passed through the gate of death, leaving behind the sweet assurance of the all-sufficiency of the grace of our Lord Jesus Christ to cheer them in the valley of death's shadow; leaving us yet over two hundred and fifty struggling for the victory. The Lord's Day school, organized soon after the church was set up, has also prospered, averaging three hundred or more in attendance.

There has never been a Lord's Day, since the commencement of the church here, but the Disciples have come together to break bread—not a week has passed without at least two prayer-meetings from house to house.

We occupy the Hall yet, but hope to get a meetinghouse of our own during this year. The Hall we use will accommodate six hundred persons comfortably, and is filled every Lord's Day. We are contributing every Lord's Day as we are prospered, and feel confident of success. The church is poor in purse, but rich in spirit, and doing nobly. May the Lord bless this noble band, and make us all a blessing. To God be all the praise for all these things he has done for us.

Knowles Shaw.

During his meeting at Wellsburg, West Virginia, which began in December, 1869, he was called home by the sad tidings of the serious illness of his eldest daughter, then about thirteen years of age. Of this meeting W.K. Pendleton, then editor of the *Millennial Harbinger*, wrote as follows:

We have just had the pleasure of spending part of a day with our earnest and devoted brother, Knowles Shaw, of Rushville, Indiana. He is holding a protracted meeting for our neighbors at Wellsburg. It has been two weeks in progress, and up to the present time over one hundred have been added to the church, most of them by baptism. He began the meeting in December, but was summoned home by the illness of a beloved daughter, a noble and lovely Christian girl, whom it pleased the Father soon to take home to himself. We have never been more strongly impressed with the power of the Christian's faith to lighten these heavy crosses than when hearing Brother Shaw speak of his bereavement. There is infinitely more than resignation; the door of the heavenly mansion seems opened to his view, and the radiance from within spans even the dark river.

> *Returning to Wellsburg, he has been preaching every evening to crowded houses, and with continually increasing interest on the part of his hearers. A prominent feature in the character of Brother Shaw is earnestness, and God is blessing it as he ever delights to do. He is a man of his own sort, and works in a way all his own. His heart is full of the love of souls, faith in the gospel, and a sense of dependence upon the divine blessing for success; and in this spirit he works, day and night from house to house, on the streets, in the offices of business, and in all places where men do congregate. His success is a fine illustration of the power of love to win the prejudiced and to unite the divided. All classes and denominations throng to hear Brother Shaw. They feel that be loves them and the truth, and will sacrifice anything lawful to save them. We hope to have still further triumphs of the truth to record before this meeting is closed.*

In the same year he held a meeting in Louisville, Kentucky, during which sixty were added; and immediately after that another in New Albany, Indiana, with twenty-six additions. In 1871 he was at Bellaire, Ohio, and twenty-nine were added as the result of his labors. And in the same year at East Cleveland, it is thus reported:

> *Our meeting of three weeks continuance has just closed, with thirty accessions, all by baptism. The circumstances were most unfavorable for a hearing. The streets were blockaded by public improvements, the spring forward, and everybody busy. Notwithstanding, the hearing was large and attentive, the audience and the interest increasing till the close. Brother Knowles Shaw did the preaching, and, by the power of his clearness and earnestness, proved fully adequate for the occasion and the circumstances. Not merely has he reaped from seed sown by our present pastor, the earnest J.B. Johnson, and other faithful laborers before him, but he has sown seed in other hearts, to bring forth fruit, we trust, to eternal life. Well and faithfully he labored, and God has given a blessed increase.*
>
> *R.R. Sloan.*

Soon after this he removed to Neosho County, Kansas, and did much for the advancement of the cause of Christ all through that region, holding meetings, gathering together the scattered Disciples, and giving an impulse to the cause that was not soon forgotten. While residing in Kansas he made frequent visits to different States; in every instance holding meetings with marked success. Among other places he preached at Galesburg, Illinois, and also in Peoria, using the Eureka tent for his meetings.

Another meeting in Missouri is thus noticed:

Clinton, Missouri, June 6, 1872.

On Lord's Day, May 12th, we commenced a protracted meeting in Clinton. Brother Knowles Shaw, famed for his great success in such meetings, was with us. He attended Sunday-school in the morning, and sang several of the fine pieces in his new book, 'Sparkling Jewels.' Then, just before preaching, he sang another piece or two, and, after service, appointed a meeting for 3 1/2 P.M. for rehearsal. Nearly all the young people of the town came, and they had a grand time, such as Clinton had never seen. At night he had singing for half an hour; then he read and commented for perhaps fifteen minutes on a passage of Scripture, and, after prayer, preached over an hour. The attendance was large and the attention profound. Such was his course throughout the meeting, day and night—half an hour's rehearsal, then reading and comment about a quarter of an hour, then the prayer and the discourse. Our audiences continued to increase until our house was filled to overflowing. Never had the like been seen in Clinton, and the people wondered that a man could talk and sing, and preach and work almost incessantly, day after day, and keep fresh and ready, and never seem tired. Our meeting lasted just three weeks, and closed with fifty-one additions to the congregation. This, considering all the circumstances, is the grandest success I have ever known.

The work done by Brother Shaw is of incalculable value. He managed by his good singing and good preaching to get the people to come. When they came once the most of them could not be kept away. We got what we have never had before in Clinton—a good hearing—and the people could see and appreciate the difference between what we really preach and what the clergy say we preach. Many who had been sprinkled in infancy, and others who had been persuaded to receive it for Christian baptism, had their sandy foundation taken away, and can never rest secure until they are buried with their Lord in baptism.

J.A. Meng.

The next year we find him employed, as follows, in Iowa:

DE SOTO, January 13.

Brother Knowles Shaw has just closed a series of interesting meetings in this place. He delivered fifty-eight discourses, preaching generally twice each day. Fifty-five accessions were made to this congregation during this series of meetings. We have had a very interesting and happy meeting. The most earnest prayers and best wishes of this entire congregation go with our dear brother in Christ, who starts for his home in Kansas today. This congregation was organized a little more than two years ago. Since that time it has been strengthened by the addition of about one hundred and eighty members.

Wm. M. Roe.

The following are a few of many meetings in 1874:

KANSAS.

Knowles Shaw writes from Atchison, under date of May 15th: "I have been here four days, and a glorious meeting is already developed. Ten added. Hall crowded, and more expected."

ILLINOIS.

Knowles Shaw's meeting at Golconda continued just two weeks, and resulted in thirty-two additions —four restored, eight from the denominations, and the remainder by confession and baptism.

KENTUCKY.

Nine persons have recently been added to the congregation at Paducah. Knowles Shaw stopped at this point on his way from Golconda, Illinois, and remained five days, preaching to very large congregations.

INDIANA.

At last accounts Knowles Shaw was engaged in a protracted meeting at Bethlehem Chapel, a mission point, we believe, in Indianapolis. He was preaching to crowded houses, and twenty-eight had been added up to August 28th.

L.D. Waldo, Rockford, writes, October 28:

Knowles Shaw came to Rockford September 25, and preached and sung, and prayed and worked, as he only, of all the men I ever saw, can work, for four weeks. Thirty-two additions were made to the church; new zeal awakened in the old members; much prejudice removed from the minds of our religious neighbors, and seed sown that we hope will bring forth fruit to the glory of God. We thank God and take courage.

And again, we see:

Knowles Shaw closed a meeting at Evansville, December 14, with fifteen additions to the church.

In 1875 he returned to Indiana, making his home at Rushville; but, as ever, his labors were spread over a wide field, as we shall learn from what we give below. The Paducah *Daily Times* gives the following:

"The meeting that commenced at the Christian Church in this city, in the latter part of last week, is still progressing. The handsome church edifice of the Christian brethren, on Oak Street, is nightly crowded with attentive congregations. A deep interest seems apparent on the part of both men and women, who mingle their voices in songs of praise and thanksgiving for the blessings which the God of love has bestowed upon the children of men. The hundreds that flock to the Christian Church, every morning and evening, to

listen to the wonderful singing and preaching of the great revivalist, Elder Shaw, are unaware of the time passed in public worship, and return to their homes filled with the idea that if Elder Shaw is not a very great man he is certainly a very earnest and good man; that if he is not an accomplished scholar and an orator, according to certain fixed rules of the university and the forum, he is eloquent and enthusiastic after his own style; a natural orator, full of sentiment, and prompted in his labors for the good of mankind by what he believes to be 'the truth, the whole truth, and nothing but the truth.' Honest in his opinions, liberal in his feelings, of ardent temperament, and of manners entirely different from any and every body else in the world, Elder Shaw impresses himself upon his audience with peculiar strength and force. Filled with the spirit of his sublime calling, with heart overflowing with love and kindness for his fellow-man, it is no wonder that his presence in our midst is deemed a source of so much delight to our fellow-citizens of every denomination...

There was an immense audience at the Christian Church, on Oak Street, last night, to listen to the splendid singing and eloquent preaching of the 'Singing Evangelist,' Knowles Shaw. Every available seat was occupied; the altar, and even the pulpit, crowded with a delighted assemblage of our citizens, both young and old. Mr. Shaw has produced a decided sensation in this community. Never, in the history of the Christian Church of this city, has the interest been surpassed to listen to the music of the hymns of Sankey and Bliss, and other productions of the sacred muses. Mr. Shaw is an orator entirely like himself, and unlike any one else that we have ever heard of. He is sui generis in every undeniable respect; he is emphatically Knowles Shaw, and no one else. Some portions of his sermon, last evening, would have done honor to the head and heart of the great Spurgeon or Bascom, or to Bishop Elliott. Crowds nightly flock to the Christian Church to listen to our distinguished visitor, whose powers of song and speech seem inexhaustible. Many who go to scoff, remain to pray.

> *We predict that great good must follow the efforts of Mr. Shaw to advance the cause of his Master among men...*
>
> *By 7 o'clock last night the church was packed, and great numbers were compelled to go away, not being able to get in. We have never seen a deeper solemnity nor better behavior in a house so crowded. The first thirty minutes was spent in singing, and in some of the songs it seemed as if every one in the house was singing. A great number asked Mr. Shaw to sing 'Drifting Away,' which he did, after making a few heart-touching remarks about interference. Mr. Shaw then sang, by request, 'The half has never been told.' The sermon, last night, was short, but we heard many say that it was the best sermon Mr. Shaw has preached. Numbers stood up without moving during the entire sermon. From the number of verses read and quoted from the Bible, it could be truly said that the word was preached. At the close of the sermon Mr. Shaw made one of his strongest appeals to the unconverted. The congregation then sang, 'Free from the law.' Seven or eight persons went forward to unite with the church, and a number of others were deeply interested. Baptism will be attended to tonight at the close of the meeting.*
>
> *We are told that the morning meetings are largely attended. Mr. Shaw's morning talks are short and pointed, and addressed especially to Christians. There are no useless speculations in Mr. Shaw's preaching, no new theory; it is the 'Old, old story,' told by one who believes it and loves to tell it.*

Shaw himself reports from other points as follows:

> *I closed a good meeting in Ohio, Bureau County, Illinois, after two Lord's Days' continuance, with sixty-eight additions—sixty of these by confession and baptism. This was a grand triumph for truth. Brother A. Ross preaches for them, and will help the new members along. Commenced here in Sterling our tent-meeting Friday last, and though at first but about one hundred and fifty came out, we now have the tent filled. Lord's Day and last night there were two thou-*

sand or more. Pray for us. Will remain here three weeks or more.

I have just returned from a short visit to the church in Manilla, Rush County, where I spent eight days, preaching twice each day. The immediate result was nineteen baptisms, and a general stirring up of the community. This church used to meet at Mud Creek, and there I obeyed the gospel twenty-two years ago. It is a joy to meet old friends, but sad that so many are gone.

F.M. Kirkham, Centreville, Iowa, writes:

The church in this place has just closed a meeting of twenty-five days' continuance, rich in results—there having been added one hundred and three.

Everything was ripe for a glorious meeting. The church having occupied, only a few weeks before the meeting commenced, for the first time, their beautiful and commodious new chapel, for the erection of which the brethren and friends had contributed freely and nobly of their means, thereby enlisting their sympathies in spiritual things, were thus to some extent ready to hear all things commanded by God.

Brother Knowles Shaw did the preaching, delivering, in all, fifty-one discourses, doctrinal and practical, in his peculiarly clear, earnest, and eloquent manner, and awakening a religious interest in this community such as we have never had before. His day discourses were directed mainly to the brethren, and have done much to build them up in the faith, hope, and love of the gospel, and to strengthen and confirm the previous labors of the pastor of the church.

This has been a meeting of peculiar interest and power, not only in its results here, but throughout this region—many brethren from different parts of the country, and even adjoining counties, lending their presence, and contributing otherwise to its success, and carrying home with them its leavening influences.

Other reports:

INDIANA.

Knowles Shaw remained at Greencastle three weeks, during which time thirty-four persons were added to the church. The meeting was continued by Brother Laughlin, but we have not yet learned the result. From Greencastle Brother Shaw went to Terre Haute.

Knowles Shaw recently held a few days' meeting at Clarksburg, during which eight persons were baptized and the church much encouraged.

The aggregate of additions was four hundred and sixteen; the number of which was greatly increased during the year by his labors at other points. Although without a full report of his work and its results, we have fuller reports of the year 1876 than of any preceding it. A partial report is given below, much of it in the words of the laborer himself:

Chicago, Illinois, January 17.

I have just returned from Buchanan, Michigan, where I spent three weeks by special permission of the congregation here, for which I am laboring. There were two hundred and twenty-six added in all, two hundred and twelve by confession and baptism. On New Year's Day there were thirty-six, and on the first Lord's Day in the new year twenty-five additions. This, for the time engaged, is the crowning work of my life. The house used was the Advent Church, because larger and more central. Indeed, the work was a union effort, by the Advents and our church. A permanent union of the churches is anticipated. A committee of eight from each church have already agreed on the basis of union, and our congregation adopted it immediately, but there were thirteen of the Advent Church opposed, and they adjourned to hold another meeting to further consider the matter. The basis is our old plea: Christ the foundation; faith, repentance, confession and baptism the way to get on the foundation, and Christian character the test of fellowship, allowing all to enjoy their opinions. The name agreed upon

> *for the church is, 'Church of Christ.' The cause in Buchanan is now in a most prosperous condition.*
>
> *I commenced a work here, yesterday, to continue for some days, as circumstances may require. We are progressing here in every way slowly; some accessions nearly every meeting by letter, and several baptisms since I came. The work on West Side is doing well. I preach there every Sunday at 3 P.M. Their Sunday-school attendance is good—one hundred and sixty-three yesterday. Our Sunday school numbered one hundred and fifty-six.*
>
> Knowles Shaw.

A month later he writes from Chicago:

> *Our work goes on gloriously here—fifty additions to date, and more are expected. House filled, and five added last night. Pray for us. The gospel triumphs over all error. We will continue another week.*

Soon after we find the following:

> *I recently spent a little over three weeks in Rush County, Indiana, my old home, where I preached, while resting, thirty-two discourses, and had forty-four additions—thirty of these at Ben Davis Creek and fourteen at Little Flat Rock. First meeting, ten days; the other, four days. So I rested during my vacation from city work.*
>
> Knowles Shaw.

> *Chicago, Illinois, September 25, 1876.*
>
> *I closed a two-weeks' meeting on the 22nd, at New Bedford, McDonough County, Illinois, with twenty-five additions, besides raising money to pay off all liabilities incurred in the erection of their new and beautiful house of worship just finished.*
>
> Knowles Shaw.

In October he began a meeting in Covington, Kentucky. One of the city papers mentioned it as below:

The meetings conducted by Elder Knowles Shaw, at Fifth Street Christian Church, in this city, have passed through four weeks, with ninety-six additions. The audience last night was larger than on any previous occasion; all the seats were closely packed. The aisles, and all the vacant spaces around the pulpit and in the gallery, were filled with hearers, and the hallway outside the main audience-room was crowded with people who could hear, but could not see the preacher.

This great audience paid the most profound attention, and the speaker well repaid them in one of his most brilliant and heart-searching discourses. The labors seem to give him new powers. He exhibits no signs of weariness or weakness, but preaches and sings as though he were just entering upon a new meeting.

The pastor of the church writes as follows:

Covington, November 10.

Brother Shaw took leave of us on Wednesday evening last, carrying with him the good wishes of all. There were additions at the last meeting, and I believe there were many more 'almost persuaded.' He removed some prejudice, sowed a large quantity of very good seed, and, in addition, reaped a harvest of over one hundred souls; thus making our church record larger than it ever has been. The audiences were large throughout, sometimes immense, and the best of order prevailed. Brother Shaw sings well, and the work moved on. He is a good protracted meeting preacher, not easily discouraged, and physical strength equal to any emergency. He preached and sung for us nearly five weeks, and his voice—always loud and strong—was as clear at the close as at the beginning. He is willing to do all the work if necessary, and, like Alexander the Great, grieves that there are not more worlds to conquer. He is all zeal and activity, and exerts unsparingly his great energies to get people into the church. He refers, with apparent pride, to the multitudes that have joined under his preaching. He is never still, in the meeting-house or out of it; talks constantly about the meeting and the work he is doing; often alludes in his sermons to things which have transpired in his own experience, and sometimes with magical effect. He speaks with great boldness and plainness; he uses a broad-ax rather than a smoothing-plane; his sword is two-edged, and cuts down everything before it. Popular vices receive no countenance at his hands. Sectarianism and error in every form receive his unqualified denunciation. He preaches the old Jerusalem, Pentecostal gospel faithfully, and tells sinners with great emphasis what they must do to be saved. He exhorts Pedobaptists and Affusionists to obey the gospel, assuring them that their baptism is nothing. I have heard none of our preachers that planks matters down any plainer and more uncompromisingly than Brother Shaw. I had my fears from what I had heard that he was not quite sound on some of these questions, but my fears were soon dissipated. Brother Franklin himself, in his palmiest days, was never more tenacious for the integrity of first principles. I am glad to be able to bear this testimony. If Brother Shaw belonged to that class who pretend to believe the Reformation a failure, and who, therefore, preach liberalism, progression away from Jerusalem and the New Testament, anything, everything, and nothing, and smooth things over to get the good will of the sects, he might do us, as a people, immense harm. But he satisfied us here that he is a sound gospel preacher. If he preaches everywhere the same way he preached here, he will pass current for a good 'Campbellite,' which, being interpreted, means one who believes and practices as did Christ and his apostles.

We feel thankful to God for his abundant mercies, and shall endeavor, by his grace, to make ourselves still more worthy of his love. Our additions are mostly young people—some few middle-aged and heads of families — and all of an excellent and promising class. The prospect is good yet for more, and we will be somewhat disappointed if others do not come soon.

P.B. Wiles.

And a correspondent of the *Standard* says:

> *Covington, October 31.*
>
> *I regret that you have not been able to attend our meeting, now in its fourth week, to hear the sermons and songs, and see Brother Shaw's methods, so that you, from actual knowledge and observation, could have made a true, full, and faithful report.*
>
> *I am sure that Brother Shaw has been greatly misunderstood, misrepresented, and undervalued. I myself had a great prejudice against him, produced by representations that his mannerisms were objectionable, his methods frivolous, and his preaching chaffy, and the effects produced evanescent. A greater injustice could not be done him than so to represent him and his work. I have been a member of the Christian Church nigh unto forty years; I have heard all the old preachers—Campbells, Scott, Burnet, Franklin, Errett, Johnson, Moss, Creath, Gano, Smith, Hopson, McGarvey, Lard, and a host of others, and now I find Brother Shaw preaching the same gospel, and, by his zeal, devotion, logic, pathos, and fervent love for Christ and his cause, moving, by the help of God, multitudes to cry out, 'What shall we do to be saved? He is peculiarly adapted to the work of an evangelist, and should everywhere receive the cordial co-operation of all Christian workers.*
>
> *I wish he could remain and work in Kentucky five years. I believe he would warm up, and make alive again, all the elements in all our churches, and push forward the grand movement fifty years.*
>
> *John F. Fisk.*

Brother Shaw speaks thus of his last meeting for the year:

> *Jackson, Tennessee, December 18.*
>
> *Our work at South Bend closed on the 6th, with thirty additions. Truly, for so short a work, this was great success, under existing circumstances. The time only little over two weeks. Large congregations from the first. Compelled to get*

the Opera House after the first week. There are true and noble Christians in South Bend. A letter from there gives encouraging news. Prayer-meeting large, prospects good. I have been here one week—two added. Will remain another week. I go next to Columbus, Mississippi, by the 28th, and to Memphis by 15th of January.

Knowles Shaw.

The aggregate additions from the above reports are five hundred and thirty, and, as stated, the reports by no means include all the results of the year.

Imperfect as the reports are, however, few men have made such a record as we have given in a single year.

During this year, too, he was pastor of the church at Chicago, to which about one hundred persons were added. He preached, while in the city, three times every Lord's Day, except when he preached four times, and in two cases only twice. Although his work was successful, when compared with that of others, he felt that his real work was that of an evangelist, and he accordingly decided to make that his chief work, and resigned his position on the 4th of September. The impression produced by reading such a record as the above is more like that produced by a life, than a single year of earnest and faithful labor.

Chapter Five

His Love for the Lost—Blue Dick—Labors in the Murphy Movement—Singing "Lambs of the Upper Fold" at a Childs Funeral.

Brother Shaw was an enthusiast, but his enthusiasm was the farthest possible remove from fanaticism. It had its origin in deep and earnest convictions, which found an outlet in ceaseless effort for the welfare of humanity. The world lying in wickedness was not a mere theory; to him it was a solemn, an awful fact. He realized the danger of his fellow- men, and warned them of their peril, and strove to snatch them as brands from the burning. Every human soul was, in his eyes, a gem of priceless worth—condition and circumstances went for nothing—under all surroundings, favorable or otherwise, he saw an immortal soul to be saved or lost. Where others saw only a helpless, wretched, hopeless outcast, he saw one for whom Christ died, who, under the influence of the gospel, might be cleansed from sin, have fruit unto holiness, and the end everlasting life. He remembered that the Master came to seek and save the lost; that his condescension led him to seek and lift up the lowly, and this led him to care for the souls of those for whom none else on earth seemed to care.

Sometimes his brethren, with less faith in God and humanity than himself, would discourage his attempts to reform and save some who seemed utterly abandoned and vile; but such opposition only added to his zeal, and made him increase his efforts in behalf of those whom men had forsaken, and who deemed themselves forsaken of God.

Among those who called forth his deep sympathy was one who is still living—changed beyond all that was at one time thought possible, and whom we trust will be one of the brightest stars in Brother Shaw's crown of rejoicing. He was holding a meeting at some point on the Ohio River, where it was necessary for him to cross frequently. The first night of his meeting he went down to the river, but found the only ferryman to be a poor, ragged, besotted wretch, no hat on his head, his hair matted, his whole person filthy in the extreme, and giving evidence that he was even then under the influence of drink. His appearance was so forbidding, and his condition such that he was doubtful as to whether it would be safe to entrust himself in a frail skiff with such a ferryman, and had there been any other and safer means of getting across he would have availed himself of it. But there was no other chance, and with some misgivings as to the result he entered the boat. He soon found that, though under the influence of liquor, he knew how to manage his skiff, and feeling at ease on that matter, he began to talk with him. He asked him his name.

"Blue Dick," was the reply.

"But," said Shaw, "that is not really your name."

"Well," said he, "if I have any other, it has been so long since I heard it, I have almost forgotten what it is."

Changing the subject abruptly, he asked, "Why don't you quit drinking?"

"I can't," said the poor wretch.

"Yes, you can," replied Shaw.

Wondering that a stranger should take any interest in him, he said, "Mister, do you think I could?"

"Of course you can," said Shaw, in a kind and assuring manner.

The poor fellow sat for some time in silence. It was long since any word of sympathy, interest, or encouragement had fallen upon his ear, and the kind words of the stranger reached the heart which all his neighbors thought had ceased to feel. Deeply moved, he looked up and said, earnestly:

"Mister, do you really think I could quit drinking?"

"Have you a wife and children?"

In a voice choked with emotion, and weeping bitterly, he said that he had. The way was now open. Shaw told him he was a preacher, and asked him to come and hear him.

"Why," said he, "you would not let such a one as me come; and if *you* were willing, others would not like to see me there."

Shaw urged him to come, assured him that he should be welcome; that instead of being out of the reach of mercy, that it was such as he that Jesus came to save. Tenderly and earnestly he besought him to change his course, until the poor ferryman began to think that there might be hope even for him. On reaching the other side, Shaw paid him his fare, and, as he did so, he pointed to a saloon that was near, and Said, "I do not like the idea of this money going to such a place as that; can't you promise me that you will not drink any tonight, and I will come back, and you shall take me over the river again."

Blue Dick gave the required promise and they parted; the preacher going to the house of God, and the ferryman, with emotions such as had not stirred in his heart for years, standing in deep thought by the rapid river under the watching stars.

After meeting, Brother Shaw went down to the river, found Blue Dick waiting for him, showing by his manner that he had kept his promise not to drink. He gave him a few words of encouragement, and obtained his promise that he would come and hear him preach the following night. Great was the astonishment of many to see Blue Dick at church, and greater still to see the preacher, who had seen him come in and drop into the first empty seat that he found near the door, come up to him, take him by the hand, speak a few kind words to him, and ask him to come again. Night after night he came, and the warm hand of the preacher never failed to give that of Blue Dick a friendly grasp, and the fitting words spoken did not fail to strengthen the new purposes that were beginning to take shape in his mind. The coming of the one, and the marked attention shown him by the preacher, led some of the brethren to fear, yes *fear*, that this poor outcast might offer himself for membership; and they even expressed their fears to Brother Shaw, and predicted that it would ruin the church if one such as he should attempt to enter the fold. Brother Shaw, however, did not fail to show, in their loveliest colors, the tenderness and compassion of Him who came to give hope to the hopeless, to seek and to save the lost. The lost sheep, and the wayward, wretched, ruined prodigal seemed to point to Blue Dick, and Blue Dick himself began to think they meant him; and one night, when the preacher, with even more than his wonted earnestness, urged the despairing and lost to come to Christ as their only hope, Blue Dick rose to come forward and accept the gospel offer. The preacher went half-way down the aisle to meet him; angels doubtless, too, at that moment gave expression to their joy in glad song, and He who died to save the lost was, doubtless, glad to see that the lost was found. But, alas! while there was joy in heaven, the coming of poor Blue Dick to confess his Lord, to strive to lead a better life, did not send a thrill of joy through the church; some there were who, like the elder son in the parable, thought that the returned wanderer would never be other than a disgrace to the family, thought that Blue Dick had gone too far to retrace his steps, and that his newly-formed resolutions would be broken on the very first invitation to take a drink, and that he would soon sink to even a lower depth, if possible, than before. Such was the feeling of opposition with regard to him that Brother Shaw did not take his confession and baptize him for several days, feeling, doubtless, that until he could change their views on the subject, that their coolness would repel and discourage, rather than help and save. Before the meeting closed, to the wonder of the whole community, Blue Dick made a public confession of his faith in Christ, was baptized, and by his consistent life soon disarmed whatever of objection remained, and was regarded as a standing proof of the power of the gospel.

Years passed by; the faithful evangelist revisited the same place. Blue Dick was no longer there; he was transformed into Brother George M., one of the best members of the church; he was living in a comfortable home, surrounded by a loving and happy family, with every mark of neatness and thrift about them. As soon as Brother Shaw had entered this happy Christian home, he who had been Blue Dick said: "Brother Shaw, kneel down and thank God for what he has done for me, that I, who when you met me was a poor, miserable, drunken sinner, have been lifted up, and, by the mercy of God, am what I am today." Down they knelt; preacher, husband, wife, and children, all, all wept; but they were tears of joy; and when they parted it was in the glad hope of meeting in that blessed land where no partings shall be.

The fact that Shaw, at one period of his life, had contracted a taste for strong drink, and had strength and resolution enough to abandon at once and forever that which had so nearly been his ruin, gave him great power over such as had been enslaved by the same appetite. His own escape from the snare made him feel great interest and hope for the escape of others; and to such his own case was a proof that, though they had wandered so long and far in the path of criminal self-indulgence, a return was not impossible. He not only approved the various temperance reforms which sprang up, but became a bold and fearless advocate of them. He did not wait for them to become popular, but was always in the advance of every movement upon that question. His labors in the temperance cause alone would have made him a man of mark, and yet his work in that field was only an episode in the labors of his life. He was quite prominent in what is known as the "Murphy Movement." Indeed, few men did more to further it than he. He was never more at home than when before immense temperance mass meetings; hundreds have signed the pledge under the influence of one of his impassioned appeals.

In quite a number of places, North and South, he inaugurated the "Murphy Movement," and thousands under his labors were led to renounce the rule of the demon drink. During the last few months of his life he enlisted about fifteen hundred persons into the temperance army; gaining one hundred and fifty at a single meeting only a few days before his death.

While engaged in a meeting in Kentucky he was greatly prostrated by his excessive labors. The sister at whose house he was stopping urged him to take some brandy, but he declined to touch it. The lady had some sent to his room and placed in his reach while he was asleep. When he awoke and found it so near him his old desire came back with fearful violence; he arose from his bed, fell upon his knees, and asked God for strength to overcome it, and, taking the bottle to the lady, told her how his long-slumbering appetite had been aroused, and begged her never again to place such a temptation in the way of any one who had ever been under the influence of that monster evil.

Being able to hold in check the fearful craving that early indulgence had created, gave him great power in persuading others, who had lost all confidence in their ability to control their appetites, to make a struggle to do so; and not a few did so successfully. Many of his religious converts were persons who had fallen into this fearful vice, but in his esteem none were so fallen as to be beyond hope of recovery; and many such today are worthy and useful members of the church, who attribute their present condition, under God, to the earnest and unselfish labors of him who had aroused them to make an endeavor to escape when hope had almost died in their hearts. He seldom held a protracted meeting without delivering during its progress one or more spirited temperance lectures, which in many cases proved to be a preparative for the successful sowing in many hearts the good seed of the kingdom of God. Much of this temperance work was performed in the open air, in public squares and like places, where large crowds, who seldom visited churches, could be reached. Some of these gatherings, as for instance at the Capitol grounds in Jackson, Mississippi, and Lafayette Square, New Orleans, were such as never had been collected before for a similar purpose, and impressions were made such as will never fade away.

A striking instance of his sympathy and power to adapt himself to circumstances took place in Humboldt, Kansas. A wealthy and prominent Presbyterian family had lost an infant. Brother Shaw went, uninvited, to the funeral; the Presbyterian minister preached a funeral sermon from a text in the Old Testament, and, after the discourse, the little white coffin, covered with flowers, resting on a marble- topped table in the parlor, was opened, that the friends and heart-stricken parents might take the last look at the little unconscious sleeper. The scene was painful, the parting severe, when, amid the sobs and weeping, there fell upon their ears, in one of the tenderest, sweetest voices they had ever heard, the following words:

1. Many children, dear to us while here,
Have gone, but we are told
That our absent ones in heaven appear,
Among the saints enrolled,
As the lambs of the upper fold.

Chorus.
"For Jesus leads the tender lambs;
They are now in the land where they ne'er grow old.
How dear to us are the loving lambs,
The lambs of the upper fold.

2. I see the throng, I hear the song,
'Mid the angels on the other shore;
In the pastures green they are ever seen,
On Canaan's peaceful shore,
In the land where they weep no more.

Chorus.

3. Now let us live, to Jesus give
Our strength while young and old,
So when we are gone we may rest at home,
And walk the streets of gold,
With the lambs of the upper fold.

Chorus.

4. Then let us go to the land above,
And be with the saints enrolled,
To bear the palm and wear the crown,
And share the bliss untold,
With the lambs of the upper fold.

Chorus.

The hearts of all were hushed, and the thoughts of the stricken ones were lifted from the lifeless clay to the dear lost one, in the arms of the Good Shepherd. Shaw, entering into the spirit of the occasion, had sung one of his own sweet hymns, under circumstances that gave it great effect. It was just what the broken hearts before him needed. He was warmly thanked by the friends. The mother afterward sent her grateful acknowledgments, and a request for a copy of the verses he had sung. And she reckons among her prized treasures the "Lambs of the Upper Fold."

Chapter Six

Meeting at St. Louis—Great Interest—Reports of the Press—Results.

As one is insensibly attracted to the hero whose progress from victory to victory he traces on the page of history, so in pursuing the life of this true worker for Christ, I find my interest and admiration for him continually increasing. This, I am aware has a tendency to render me more partial than I desire to be; and yet no one could follow the current of a life like his without being similarly affected. I am glad, therefore, at this, one of the most successful periods of his career, to be able to present to the reader the views of those whose feelings had not been enlisted like my own, namely, the reporters for the press in one of the largest cities of the West, who drew the picture of his labors as they passed before them, as they would have presented before the public the work of any one in any department whatever, who was creating an interest in the public mind. A great speaker on any theme, of any party in politics, of any school of philosophy, or sect in religion, would have been treated in the same spirit of fairness, and freedom from either prejudice or undue prepossession, as was he.

This was in the city of St. Louis, in the winter of 1874. It must be remembered that Shaw did not find the clergy and churches of that great city all ready to receive him and heartily co-operate with him in his work; not even a single large and influential religious party was thus prepared. His own brethren were neither numerous nor influential, and the influence of other denominations was rather against than in favor of the effort he was about to make. St. Louis did not prepare for his coming as did the various cities of the East for the coming of Moody— making success a certainty before he came. He came almost unheralded, and the success he achieved was his own. The reports of his meeting will be given at considerable length, and from them the reader will be able to draw a pretty correct idea of the course he pursued at nearly all the places he visited. A general idea of his manner and methods may be gained, the nature of his subjects and mode of treatment may be learned to a certain extent, but it must at the same time be remembered, as well as regretted, that neither in this place nor at any other, as far as I have been able to learn, was there a full and complete report of a single discourse taken and preserved; a synopsis of several is given. They are, however, meager in the extreme; outlines which the imagination will attempt in vain to fill up. But the greatest charms of all, the looks, tones, the earnestness and pathos of the speaker, are not, and can not be described; and yet, to those who never saw and heard him, even what has been rescued from oblivion by the reporter's pencil will be read with interest and highly prized. We shall present several notices of the progress of his meeting, as nearly as possible in the order in which they appeared. They are taken from the columns of the St. Louis *Globe:*

ELDER KNOWLES SHAW.

ST. Louis, February 22, 1874.

To the Editor of the Globe:

Having learned that the great revivalist, Knowles Shaw, would preach at the Central Christian Church, Fourteenth and St. Charles Streets, on Sunday morning, I was induced to go and hear him. Mr. Shaw is certainly a man of extraordinary power, and, in my judgment, the equal, if not the superior, of Dr. Hammond in his influence over the masses. The hall in which he preached this morning was crowded, and I have seldom seen an assembly of people so deeply moved with seemingly so little effort on the part of the speaker.

Mr. Shaw began his discourse by saying that he was not a 'systematic' preacher; that when he first began to preach he had his first, second, and third divisions of his subject, and then he divided his first into firstly, secondly, and thirdly, and then his second and third divisions into the same general heads, and so on through to the end; that he discovered before a great while that he was not doing any good, and that if he continued to preach he must change his method, and he at once did so. He said that he had discovered that the great majority of preachers were engaged

> in trying to convert the heads of the people to the utter neglect of their hearts; that by hammering away, driving doctrines and formulas into the heads of men, the people had not only become hard-headed, but hard-hearted also. He thought that the head and the heart both needed to be converted.
>
> Having failed in his first efforts, he determined to adopt as his motto the declaration of the great Apostle to the Gentiles, and 'I determined to know nothing among you but Jesus Christ and him crucified.' He then announced as his text, 'Come, see the place where the Lord lay.'
>
> I will not attempt to give any idea even of the sermon. It was of a character that can not be even sketched. The streaming eyes of the whole audience gave evidence of the power of the man and the effectiveness of his words. If any one desires to have his soul moved to its profoundest depths, let him go and listen an hour to Mr. Shaw."

The next is as follows:

> Elder Shaw had a good audience at the hall, corner Fourteenth and St. Charles Streets, last night.
>
> Taking for his text the words, 'Ye do always resist the Holy Spirit,' he illustrated it by the case of a young man learning to drink. How the first time of entering the rum-shop he would go in at the back door and take something, and, on coming out, look carefully up and down the street to see if any one had observed his movements. By and by he gets bolder, and at last enters the front door and calls for his brandy like the rest of the crowd. At first he conceals all this from his mother. Later he doesn't care if the 'old woman' does know it. And so he goes on resisting the pleadings of his conscience till it no longer upbraids him. Resisting the Holy Spirit was explained as the resistance of any good influence, or any truth, which a man's inward consciousness might declare to him. The subject was illustrated in other ways, and then the audience moved down-stairs to a room on the first floor, where three young ladies signified their

> *choice of the good part which can not be taken away by undergoing the rite of baptism at the Elder's hands.*
>
> *Elder Shaw only arrived last Sunday, and already some forty additions have been made to the church.*

The next is at greater length.

> *The hall on the corner of Fourteenth and St. Charles Streets was crowded again last evening to hear Elder Shaw. The interest is increasing nightly, and it will soon be necessary to obtain another place in order to accommodate the audience. The subject of Elder Shaw last evening was*
>
> ### *ANGELS AND THEIR MISSION.*
>
> *This subject, he said, is supposed to belong by many to the dreamy realms of speculation, and that it evinces weakness to dwell upon such themes. If so, then we are identified with such weak ones as Noah, Job and Daniel, Isaiah, Jeremiah and Joshua, the holy apostles and martyrs and great reformers. This is a Bible theme to comfort God's children and warn the sinner. Angel means messenger; any one sent may be called an angel, but I shall speak of angels as an order of beings in God's creation.*
>
> *1. They were created angels. Many think they were once human beings and transformed into angels, but Paul says, in Hebrews 12: 'Ye are come to the spirits of just men and an innumerable company of angels,' thus drawing a line of distinction between them. He says, in Hebrews, first chapter and last verse, that the angels are ministering spirits to the heirs of salvation.*
>
> *2. Their number. Jesus said he could call more than twelve legions of angels—more than 60,000. John saw 'ten thousand times ten thousand, and thousands of thousands,' one hundred millions and more—how many he does not say. Paul says the company is innumerable.*
>
> *3. Their strength. David sang of the angels that excel in strength. The angel destroyed the first-born in all Egypt where God's direction had not been followed. An angel*

rolled away the stone from the tomb of Christ— strength to do whatever God has for them to do for man.

4. Swiftness of their flight. They came on swift wings to comfort God's people. Daniel was praying, and he says: 'Gabriel was commanded to fly swiftly, and he came to me, and touched me, and spoke to me.' He was comforted by an angel of God. If the poet is correct when he says,

> *'Tis far beyond the stars and sun,*
> *That blissful heaven above,*
> *Where we may dwell when time is done,*
> *By serving God in love,*

then the angel's flight—passing world after world, till reaching our sun, and yet 95,000,000 of miles to earth— sped through this wondrous space all in a very few minutes, for Daniel's prayer occupied but a short time, and the angel came while he was 'yet praying.' This illustrates the swiftness of their flight; but all this, though wonderful, is of but little value without a knowledge of

THEIR MISSION.

They are ministering spirits for the heirs of salvation, says Paul, Hebrews 1. Notice a few instances: Daniel in the lion's den rescued by an angel of God; Shadrach, Meshach, and Abednego, the three Hebrew children cast into the furnace. God sent his angel to comfort them, and to quench the violence of the fire. But in the New Testament we learn that an angel announced to Mary that she should be the mother of the Saviour. Soon after Christ's birth, during the edict of Herod, the angel warned Joseph and Mary to flee into Egypt for the safety of the child. After Herod's death the angel told them to return. After he grew up to manhood, and immediately after his baptism, when tempted in the wilderness, the 'angels ministered unto him.'

When in dark Gethsemane, with no human eye to watch with him, and no sympathizing friend, behold an 'angel came strengthening him.'

When arrested, Jesus said he could call more than twelve

legions of the angels. After his death and burial, on the third morning an angel rolled away the stone from the sepulcher, and told the women he was risen from the dead. After forty days, Jesus, as he was blessing his disciples, was taken up out of their sight. Two angels came down, stood by the weeping disciples, and said, 'Why stand ye gazing? This same Jesus shall come again.' They were comforted and returned to Jerusalem to await the promise.

> *Yes, Angels did his steps attend,*
> *Oft gazed and wondered where at length*
> *That scene of love should end.*

> *They saw him in the garden pray,*
> *They saw His sweat and blood;*
> *They saw his tender hands and feet*
> *Nailed to the accursed wood.*

> *They brought his chariot from the skies*
> *To bear him to his throne;*
> *And with a shout exulting cried,*
> *'The glorious work is done.'*

But angels delivered the apostles oft from prison and trouble. They wafted the spirit of poor Lazarus to the Paradise of God, and laid him in Abraham's bosom. So they ministered to salvation's heirs. 'They encamped round-about them that fear God.' How thankful should we be

> *That the angels of bliss*
> *Can bow their bright wings to a dark world like this;*
> *Can leave the bright mansions of glory above,*
> *To breathe in our bosoms some message of love.*

> *Yes, they come; on the wings of the morning they come,*
> *Impatient to bear some poor wanderer home;*
> *Some pilgrim to snatch from this stormy abode,*
> *And lay him to rest in the arms of his God.*

But the angels are

ANXIOUS FOR THE SINNER.

There is rejoicing among the angels over one sinner that

repenteth. Yes, poor sinner, they are ready to shout over your conversion to God; let them have a grand jubilee in heaven tonight.

Christ is the author of eternal salvation to all them that obey him. Come and obey the Savior; be an heir of salvation, and all the comforts of angelic ministration may be yours. The angels will be used in the last days. The harvest is the end of the world, and the reapers are the angels, to gather the tares for the fire, but the wheat for the garner of the Lord. May you all be found in that day on the side of Jesus; to insure this, enlist in his army. Now, come tonight.

There are reporters here taking down my poor scattering words, my weak and imperfect appeals to you to come to Jesus; but there are other reporters here—the angels of God are here —and they are taking note of emotions that crowd your hearts, and they will report them to the loving Jesus. They are here to waft the glad news of your return to God, when all heaven will rejoice. Will you come to Jesus, and come now?

ELDER SHAW'S REVIVAL CONTINUES TO INCREASE IN INTEREST.

The meetings at the Central Christian Church, Fourteenth and St. Charles Streets, are growing in interest. The hall was filled to its utmost capacity, many persons standing in the aisles, who were unable to obtain seats.

Mr. Shaw, as his custom is, before the regular service, read a portion of Scripture—Luke, 19th chapter— and made some practical comments respecting the necessity of sinners coming to Jesus. He said, if sinners would see Jesus, they must do as Zaccheus did, get above the world. They must persevere and press through difficulties, and Jesus will go with him and 'sup with him.' After singing and praying the speaker introduced his subject—

THE GLORIOUS GOSPEL,

Taking as his text 2 Corinthians 4:3-4: 'But if our gospel be hid, it is hid to them that are lost: in whom the god of this world hath blinded the minds of them which believe not, lest the light of the glorious gospel of Christ, who is the image of God, should shine unto them.'

All God's works are glorious, from the atom to the archangel. The flower that blooms at our feet, the grassy carpet of the earth, the songsters in the air, the beautiful stars in the vaulted heavens, all, to the Bible student, proclaim the glory of God. So that while the gloomy lie of the Atheist goes the rounds, that there is no God, every pulsation of his own heart, every atom of his own nature, everything around, above, and beneath contradict him, saying, 'There is a God, and he is thy Maker.' And yet there is one scene around which cluster the chief glory of God—one wreath, the most glorious of all—and that is the wreath around the cross of Christ. Let us consider some of the reasons for calling the gospel glorious. First, on account of its origin. It came from heaven; it is not a plant of earthly renown. It author, Christ, came from the bosom of the Father. The all-glorious Saviour, by whom all worlds were made, is the center, soul, and circumference of the gospel. His death, his burial, his resurrection, as Paul saith —1 Corinthians 15—are the great themes of the gospel. But some will say, 'This gospel came not from God.' Then whence came it—from man? Did bad men make it? No; they would not condemn themselves on its every page. Bad men would not like to write their own eternal death warrants. If bad men made it, they have made the best book ever written. When I gather figs from thistles, grapes from the thorn- tree, and dip sweet waters from a bitter fountain, I may believe that bad men made the gospel. Did good men make it? No.

ALL MEN MAY MAKE MISTAKES.

Good men may err sometimes; but a good man will not lie willingly and die for his falsehood. All those whose names appear upon its page say it came from God. Holy men of old spake as they were moved by the Spirit. The apostles spake the words the Holy Spirit taught them. Yes, glorious in its origin; glorious as its divine Author. The gospel is glorious on account of its rarity. It is the only thing of the kind in all God's universe. If diamonds were as plentiful as grains of corn they would not be valuable. 'Tis their rarity that is the reason of their value. The gospel is the only seed from which the Christian grows; the only plan of salvation for a lost world; the only proclamation of pardon and promise of life eternal in all the realms of God known to mortals. Let us illustrate. See that mother bending over that little pair of shoes and those little dresses in yonder drawer. Her tears drop like rain. What meaneth this? Mother, will you sell those little shoes? No, no, she replies. Will you sell those little dresses? No. Why not? She answers, there are no other little shoes my darling baby's feet ever wore; no other little dresses she used to wear. Yes [here Mr. Shaw sung the song],

> *Put aside the little dresses*
> *That our darling used to wear,*
> *She will need them on earth never,*
> *She has climbed the golden stair.*
>
> *She is with the happy angels,*
> *And I long for one sweet kiss;*
> *Where those little feet are waiting,*
> *In the realms of perfect bliss;*
>
> *For the angels whisper that our darling*
> *Is in the land of love so fair,*
> *That her little feet are waiting*
> *Close beside the golden stair.*
>
> *Kiss those little curly tresses,*
> *Cut from her bright golden hair:*
> *Do the angels kiss our darling*
> *In that world of love so fair?*
>
> *Oh, we pray to meet our darling*
> *For a long, long, fond embrace,*

*Where her little feet are waiting,
And we'll see her face to face.*

"Were the gospel obliterated it could not be reproduced, and man would soon fall back into terrible heathenism. Glorious in its rarity. Next, it is glorious in its simplicity. Its facts are easily understood; they are three: The death, the burial, the resurrection of Jesus Christ (1 Corinthians 15:1-4). Its commands are simple and readily comprehended; there are three to induct us into the kingdom here: Believe in Christ (Romans 10:9-10. John 3:18); repent of all your sins (Acts 17:30. Luke 13:5); be baptized (Mark 16:16. Acts 2:38. Acts 10:48, etc.). These several commands must be obeyed to finish the work (See 2 Peter 1:5-9). All these are easily understood. The gospel is glorious on account of its simplicity. I am often amused, and sometimes pained, to hear ministers making such terrible efforts to display their learning, instead of using it to make a matter so plain that it can not be misunderstood. They make it so mysterious with their highfalutin, toploftically, grandiloquent superlatives that it can't be comprehended. What think you of a preacher who says, 'A city situate on an eminence is conspicuous,' instead of 'A city set on a hill cannot be hid?' The gospel is plain. The feeblest intellect accountable to God can comprehend it. It is perfectly adapted to all responsible beings.*

Fourth and last: The gospel is glorious in its influence. This influence is threefold; it is enlightening. 'The entrance of thy word,' says the Psalmist, 'giveth light.' Said Jesus to Saul of Tarsus: I have appeared unto you to send you to the Gentiles, to open their eyes, to turn them from darkness to light. In nature, no light no life: so in grace. 'It is pure, enlightening the eyes.' It is controlling in its influence. How many are here whom the gospel has controlled; bringing them from awful sinfulness to the happy state of the justified! (See Acts 2:23, to close of the chapter; also 1 Corinthians 6, 9, 10, 11.) These were all conquered by the gospel." Here Mr. Shaw gave several touching cases of conversion under his own observation. One of the most striking was that of "Blue Dick," a notorious drunkard, redeemed, happiness brought to wife and children, and to the poor man's own heart, and to society. These were related with thrilling effect. "Lastly, the gospel's influence is comforting in its promises, pardon, the gift of the Holy Spirit, and a home in heaven. It promises the rebel sinner pardon and peace; it offers to the homeless a home beyond the shadows of the grave; to the tempest-tossed mariner on life's boisterous ocean a quiet haven, into which his vessel may sail for safety. To the weary, foot-sore traveler it offers a rest after the journey is past. Oh, glorious gospel! It gives us back our loved ones, now departed. It is balm to the wounded soul. It wipes the mourner's tears away, and gives us peace; opens the gate to the soul when the night of death comes; ushers us into that blessed society of the angels and all the holy throng. Sinner, will you accept this glorious gospel? Come to the Savior; no longer delay. He calls you now; has been calling long; open your hearts and let him come in. Now, while the Father is smiling, while Jesus is pleading, while angels are ministering, while glory is beaming, while the glorious gospel is calling, and Christians praying for you, come; come now, a warm heart's welcome will be given you. This offer will not stand forever; the time will come when these opportunities will be yours no more. Who will come?"

ELDER KNOWLES SHAW AT MASONIC HALL.

The interest in these meetings does not flag in the least. There was a large audience present in the morning, and at night the large hall was literally full. We have seldom seen such marked attention in so large an audience. At the close of the morning services five or six persons were received into the church. The meetings will be continued through the week at the hall on Fourteenth and St. Charles Streets.

It is Mr. Shaw's custom to sing while the people are gathering, and this morning, although suffering from cold, he sang several songs from his own book, called 'Sparkling Jewels.' After these songs he read a portion of Scripture, and commented on it—particularly the text, 'Receive ye one another, without regard to difference of opinion.' He said that opinions are based on reason—human reason is fallible, and ought not, under any circumstances, be set up as conditions of fellowship. He illustrated his point by a number of examples, and closed this lesson with an exhortation to bear with one another; that none other than a selfish spirit would insist on the adoption of his opinions to the exclusion of all others. Such action on the part of any one demonstrated that he valued his own opinions more than he valued the wisdom of God and of Christ, who has taught us to receive one another in love, without regard to these differences. God is judge—who art thou, who condemns? Every man stands or falls before his own Master.

The subject for the morning was

THE MEDIATION OF CHRIST,

From the text in Second Timothy, second chapter and fifth verse—'For there is one God and one Mediator between God and man—the man Christ Jesus.' Not gods many and mediators many, nor, as we have it in our day, one God and many mediators—not that. There is one God, and there is one Mediator, and that one Mediator is Jesus the Christ.

The necessity for mediation grew out of the fall of man. Before man sinned he communed with God directly—without a 'middle one,' or a 'between man.' How long this happy age lasted we know not, nor is it important that we should. It continued until man sinned; then came the necessity of mediation. Man could no longer approach God in his own person; he has become defiled by sin. For four thousand years the mediation was more or less imperfect. Man approached God through the sacrifice of an animal presented by one appointed and set apart for that duty. In the patriarchal age the father of the family officiated for himself and family. But these were but men, and imperfect men besides, who had first to offer SACRIFICE FOR THEMSELVES, *And then for the people, and the sacrifice itself had no consciousness of sin, and the mediation was necessarily imperfect. Then came the Mosaic dispensation. Moses was mediator between God and the people, and interceded for them when they sinned. Afterward the tribe of Levi was set apart to the priest's office, and offered the sacrifices for the people; but these were only men, and imperfect men, too, the same imperfect mediators, the same sacrifices having no consciousness of sin, could not make the comers thereunto perfect. Angels partook not of the nature of man, and did not, therefore, possess the requisite qualifications. There is one Mediator, between God and man, the man Christ Jesus. This leads to the inquiry respecting the characteristics of a perfect mediator. He must be acquainted with both parties; must understand the nature and disposition of both parties; he must understand the nature of the difficulty; he must possess the confidence of both parties; must be related to both. These qualifications are all possessed by the Lord Jesus Christ. He is divine, and he is human; consequently related to both parties.*

HE WAS WITH GOD"

He has been with man. He is acquainted with the requirements of the Divine government; he knows the weaknesses of the human nature, for he was human; he knows our frames; he experienced our sorrows, our tears, our disappointments, our anxieties; he has felt and he understands the depth and strength of the sympathies and affections of the human heart; he passed through them all, from the cradle to the grave. There are those who imagine that children do not have troubles and trials and disappointments, but they do, and Jesus sympathizes with them as he does with children of a larger growth; he took them into his arms and blessed them. He then gave several cases to illustrate the deep affections and anxious solicitude of the little ones, and the way in which parents often treat their little ones and crush out these emotions and loves; and sang two verses of a little song with thrilling effect.

Jesus sympathizes with the young. He sympathizes with the race in every condition of life. He began at the base of the hill. He passed through every condition in life. He saw it all. He felt it all. He stooped to the lowest. None too low for Jesus' sympathy—none so high he can not reach. With one hand he lays hold on the throne of God, with the other the human race, and thus he mediates peace. He has purchased your peace by the sacrifice of himself. God is waiting for the sinner's return. Will you not accept of the mediation of Christ, and become reconciled to God?"

We close these extracts with the following:

Elder Shaw preached to another large audience last evening. Since the commencement of his meetings the interest has been steadily on the increase and many souls have been converted from the ways of sin to a belief in future salvation. After the services last evening a number of converts were baptized. We give below a synopsis of his sermon. The text was taken from Amos, fourth chapter and twelfth verse: 'Prepare to meet thy God.'

The meeting with God is inevitable, else the warning had never been given. It is a solemn warning, and admonitions come to us every day, every hour, every moment. We have this warning in the falling leaves, our dying friends; everything sounds out a solemn warning, yet thousands act as if they never expected to meet God. Yet Paul says: 'All things are open to him with whom we have to do.' We have to do with God, we have to meet him. All conditions must meet him, old and young, rich and poor, saint and sinner. There are no exceptions,

NO EXEMPTIONS—ALL, ALL

must meet God. I wish I could impress this solemn truth on every heart in this hall tonight. It is God's warning voice; will you heed it?

We must meet God in providence. There are those who do not believe in the providence of God, particularly in special providences, but it is found in history, in the lives of the prophets, of apostles, of every man and woman that lives, or ever has lived. Every day we live we meet God in his providences, we meet him in the death of friends, in hours of sorrow and of joy, in rejoicings and in tears,

> *In every condition, in sickness, in death,*
> *In poverty's vale or abounding in wealth,*

*And we must be **prepared** for all these. Men, when engaged in battle, prepare for the conflict; preparation is more than half the battle; we have to meet temptation and must prepare for it. Jesus prepared himself to meet death by prayer in the garden of Gethsemane. Necessity for a preparation was illustrated by examples from life; the effect of want of preparation in adversity, and the result of a preparation, was forcibly and feelingly set forth.*

WE MUST MEET GOD IN DEATH.

This is not a pleasant picture to contemplate. We love to talk of joy and pleasures and happiness, but it is not pleasant to contemplate the separation from friends, from all we love on earth; the decay of our bodies; the grave with all its darkness—but these are realities and must be met. We must meet God in judgment; that day which shall reveal the secrets of all hearts. The motives of the heart will be the basis of that judgment—not from mere outward appearance. All sins unforgiven will stand out in all their blackness and terribleness to condemn us forever. A preparation is absolutely necessary. Think not to leave it off till death shall come; do not wait for God to do more. Till you have done your duty God will do no more; he has done nearly all. Just a little for you to do —do it without delay.

THE PREPARATION—WHAT IS IT?

We find man unregenerated, unprepared in heart, in the purpose of his life, and in his relation or state. How came he so? When man dwelt in Eden pure and holy, he was first induced to unbelief through falsehood preached by Satan, who negatived God's word—this unbelief ruined the heart—then this bad heart suggested a change of will from good to bad, or repentance from God in a resolve to disobey God's command; then when unbelief had ruined the heart, and a resolve to do wrong had ruined man's purpose or will, then an overt act of disobedience, in eating the forbidden fruit, was the ruin of man's state or relation. On account of this act man was driven out of Eden.

Now, if belief of falsehood or unbelief of the truth ruins the heart, the belief of truth or faith will purify the heart. Paul says, 'God purifies the heart by faith.' After a preparation of the heart by faith, then the will is prepared by

REPENTANCE TOWARD GOD.

This is induced by godly sorrow and leads to reformation of life. And as man is wrong in his relation, he must now file his intention to become a citizen of Christ's kingdom, by a public confession of Christ as the Divine Saviour, the only atoning sacrifice for sin, after which his state is changed, by the 'oath of allegiance' in holy baptism, into the name of Father, Son, and Holy Spirit. This preparation is finished by a life of piety and prayerfulness, thus becoming assimilated to the character of God. In all this we are aided, instructed, and guided by the Holy Spirit, who enables us to bear the precious fruits of a holy life. Prepare now; defer not this most important of all matters. The solemn warning is heard from all our dying friends. Your own hearts tell you we must prepare soon, or meet God unprepared. Oh, how solemn the thought— to be ushered into the presence of the Holy God and Jesus Christ without due preparation. Begin by giving your heart to Christ; then you may die with your face heavenward, with all the rich promises of the gospel to cheer you as you pass through the valley.

As the result of these labors one hundred and fifty persons were added to the church, many weak and weary ones strengthened and refreshed, and seed sown in many hearts, of which eternity alone will tell the harvest.

Chapter Seven

Anecdotes—A Change of Heart Wanted—Scoffer Silenced— Danger of Immersion—Slanderer Reproved—Universalists Answered—Convention Quieted—Humorous Answers.

Traveling extensively as he did, and mingling with all classes of men, he had of necessity a large and varied experience. He was everywhere at home, and equal to the occasion, whatever it might be. A volume might be filled with incidents, both amusing and instructive, but a few must suffice.

At one of his meetings a gentleman was deeply impressed, and told Shaw, with tears, that, if he could only experience a change of heart, he would confess Christ and be baptized immediately. He perceived at once the nature of the difficulty, which was the too common idea that a change of heart was a miraculous change, and not one produced by a belief in, and love for the Lord Jesus Christ. He asked him if he was sorry for his past sins? if he wanted to be a Christian? if he loved God? if he desired to go to heaven? if he believed with all his heart that Jesus Christ was the Son of the living God? To each of these questions, with the greatest earnestness and sincerity, he replied, "I do." "Then," said Shaw, "you have all the preparation needed to become a member of the Church of Christ. If your heart were changed from what it now is, you would *not* be sorry for your sins; you would *not* want to be a Christian; you would hate God; you would deny the divinity of Christ, and reject the Savior." He at once saw his mistake, confessed his faith in Christ, and was baptized.

At Dowagiac, Michigan, in 1876, the following incident took place, which shows the readiness with which he could meet and silence a scoffer. He had been invited to visit that place after his great meeting at Buchanan, Michigan, where two hundred and twenty-six additions had been made in less than a month. Of course his expected visit was the theme of common conversation, and his coming was looked for with great interest. He reached the place at a time when no one was looking for him, and at once went into a shoe store, where he found a number of persons discussing the subject of baptism, and learned from their conversation that a meeting was in progress at the church with which he expected to labor, and that additions by baptism had been made almost daily.

For some time he sat a silent listener, until one of the party said that he would go down to the river and be baptized by the "Campbellites" for a dollar. Upon this Shaw hastily took a dollar out of his pocket-book and offered it to the man who had made the above remark, saying:

"Here is your dollar; I will go down and see you baptized."

The man hesitated, and finally refused to take it; but Shaw urged him, and insisted that he should do as he had declared he would do. He then made a decided refusal, and Shaw said to him: "I knew you were lying when you made the offer, and now you are proved guilty."

"What is your name?" said the man thus accused.

"My name is Shaw," was the reply.

"What!" said the man, "Shaw the great revivalist?"

"That is what they sometimes call me," replied Shaw.

The man was greatly mortified, but, instead of cherishing hatred against him who had administered such a severe rebuke, he became one of Brother Shaw's warmest friends.

Another incident of a somewhat different character took place at DeSoto, Iowa, in the winter of 1872. Brother Shaw was conducting a series of meetings there, and the interest became intense, not only in the town, but for miles around, and scores of converts were added to the church. Among the converts was a young lady who had long been in feeble health, and was supposed to have heart disease. Some of her friends, who were greatly opposed to immersion, endeavored to convince her that immersion in her case would probably result in death. She was, however, firm in her determination, and true to her convictions of duty, and, regardless of all opposition, was immersed by Brother Shaw. The day following the report became current that she was very ill, and that her immersion would most likely result in her death. That night, as the meeting was about to close, Shaw noticed this young lady was in the audience, and, calling attention to the current report concerning her illness, he said: "This sister is not dead, nor is she seriously ill, as I will now prove." And then added: "Sister, will you please stand up on the seat that all may see you?" She complied with his request; when he said: "There she is; do you see her? Now, let those who started and circulated the false report hang their heads in shame." This scene was not forgotten, and served to increase the interest of the meeting.

During his great meeting at Buchanan, Michigan, a Methodist preacher, resident there, endeavored to change the current of public feeling, which was in Shaw's favor, by gross misrepresentations of his views. On becoming acquainted with the facts in the case, Shaw said to his audience, which was an immense one, that a certain preacher (naming him) had made some false statements, which he specified in full. He then said: "I now advertise this man as guilty of willful falsehood. May God have mercy on him." Soon after the preacher sought an interview with him, confessed the wrong he had done, and asked forgiveness. As soon as an opportunity presented itself, Shaw publicly called attention to the statements he had previously made, and said: "Brethren and friends, this man has repented of his wrong-doing and asked forgiveness. Let every one forgive him. I forgive him most freely, and may God's richest blessings rest upon him." This made a deep impression, and many were moved to tears.

He rather avoided than provoked controversy, preferring to win by kindness than conquer by force. An instance of this occurred at Humboldt, Kansas, during one of his meetings there. Two young men, Universalists, approached him on the street, and said: "We have heard, sir, that you are an able and bold defender of the Christian faith. Will you tell us what you think of hell? Is there such a place, where the wicked are tormented in fire forever and ever? We are very anxious to have that question settled, and we hope you will be able to give us some light upon it."

Shaw fixed his eyes on the ground for a moment, as in deep thought, and then looking up, replied: "I shall preach tonight, in Young's Hall, on Bridge Street, and as there may be others whose thoughts are turned in the same direction as yours, if you will come I will give my views on that subject, so that all may have the benefit of them."

This pleased them, and they soon spread the report that Knowles Shaw was going to tell what he thought about hell that night; and the result was not only every seat, but all the standing-room, was occupied.

He took as his theme the "Christian Life," and until nearly the close of the discourse did not make the slightest allusion to the subject that had brought so many there. At length he said: "Two young men accosted me on the street today and asked my opinion concerning hell. I promised to give it tonight, and, as they are here, I will proceed to do so. Within a few years past the angel of death has visited my family three times, taking one of my beloved children at each visit. I thought perhaps that the climate in which I lived had something to do with this fatality, and began to ask myself, May I not find a healthier region than where I now reside? I thought of my only daughter, her weakly constitution, her lack of vital force, and wondered if I could not find a more congenial climate, where she might be longer spared to me than I feared she would where we dwelt. I heard of Kansas, its broad prairies, its pure and healthful atmosphere. I asked every one I saw that had been there about its climate, water, and especially about its society; and the reports I heard were so favorable that I finally resolved to go. After I started, my anxiety increased, and I did not close my inquiries until I reached here. Now, why all that interest, all those inquiries? Simply because the thought of going there had taken full possession of my mind.

"About sixteen years ago I became dissatisfied with this world, its short-lived and fading pleasures, and raised the question, Is there not a better world than this? I was told that there was; that the name of that land was Heaven; that its capital was the New Jerusalem, whose streets were paved with gold; that its walls were jasper, and its gates pearl; that the river of life flowed through it; that it was a healthful clime; no sickness nor sorrow there; that its society was pure, composed of the best that the earth had ever known; and that I should be happy forever if I could enter there. The testimony was good; it came from the Son of God; Jesus had left the courts of glory, and came all the way to this sinful world of ours to tell us of his Father's house, with its many mansions; and then went back, after sealing the testimony with his blood, to prepare a place for us. I believed the testimony; and having a desire to better my condition, I started with a genuine ticket, stamped with, 'He that believeth and is baptized shall be saved.' I have been traveling in that direction ever since, making inquiries of the Book of God all the way. The nearer I get the clearer are the directions; and I am so fully persuaded that it is the best country to which a man can journey that I am constantly telling others all I know about it, and trying to get them to go with me to share its joys. As to that other country, about which those young men are so anxious to hear, I must say that I have heard of it, but the reports were so very unfavorable that I concluded it was not as good a country, and perhaps much worse than this; and as I never thought of emigrating unless it were to a better country, and to better my condition, I have thought but little about it, as I have not the least intention or desire to go there. I have therefore determined to spend my time in setting forth the glories of the better country, of heaven. We want you all to go with us; we want bold and true soldiers; hell-scared ones don't amount to much, unless you can manage to keep them scared all the way." The answer was satisfactory—there was no reason for wishing to hear more about hell.

He was ready-witted, self-possessed, had a sense of the fitness of things. If his audience seemed dull or wearied, he would stop preaching, and sing a lively song or tell an apt story, which never failed to rest and revive.

In the same way he would relieve the monotony of a business meeting, and even bring order out of confusion. He attended a convention at one time, but did not reach the place until the audience was gathered. The house was packed; no one knew him, and he took his seat among the crowd until the session was closed and the people dismissed. They were slow to leave, however; greetings took place between those who had not met for a season; the members residing there were inviting strangers to their homes; all over the house groups were engaged in conversation, and all so absorbed that no one could hear the chairman of the meeting, who had forgotten to make an important announcement, and was vainly endeavoring to gain the attention of the crowd to rectify the mistake. His efforts were all in vain. All were so interested in hearing or talking to each other that after several attempts he was obliged to give up in despair. At this juncture, Shaw got up on one of the seats and began to sing. All in the house soon had their attention attracted to the singer; those who had gone out came back to listen to the song, and long before he closed the silence was almost breathless, so charmed were all with the singer and song. When he ceased he called out, now, Mr. Chairman, you can make your announcement. He did so, and Shaw was at once the best known man at the convention.

He was not devoid of humor, as the following incidents will show. At one of his morning meetings, he had for his subject "The Shepherd and the Sheep." He said the most important thing in feeding sheep was to put something in the trough; that sheep would not come back more than twenty or thirty times when they did not get anything to eat; that the food, too, must be something that they would eat; that they would not come back many times if they found nothing but shavings in the trough; and that if the shepherd stood by and gave them a whack over the head with a club they would not be likely to come back *very* often. Now it happened that very morning he had been quite impatient with some of the sisters at rehearsal about the singing, and had scolded them severely. He went to dinner with one of them, and while eating, she said:

"Brother Shaw, you don't practice what you preach!"

"How so," said he.

"Why," she replied, "you said you must not whack the sheep on the head with a club when they come up to be fed, and you scolded us so this morning about the singing."

"Oh," said he, "I was not feeding you then; I was teaching you *to bleat*, and you *have* to whack the sheep to make them *bleat.*"

While on his way to attend the State Meeting at Emporia, Kansas, his attention was called to a man in the same car, who was utterly disgusted with the West, and with Kansas in particular; abusing the country and people in unmeasured terms; saying that the society was made up of the very scum of the Eastern States. Shaw bore it all for awhile, but at last, as if agreeing with him, said in a tone loud enough to attract attention:

"Stranger, you have told the truth this time; I have traveled all over Kansas, and I find it peopled, as you say, with the very scum of Eastern society; but it is the kind of *scum* that rises on *milk.*"

A shout of loud and long-continued laughter from all the passengers told that the arrow had reached its mark, and Kansas was vindicated.

Chapter Eight

Sketches of Several Sermons—"It is I; be not Afraid"—Pearl of Great Price — Deceitfulness of Sin — Smooth Things—Good Works—Triumphs of the Gospel.

No one could expect that Brother Shaw could produce sermons that would be models in point of taste and literary excellence. His lack of opportunity for self-improvement would forbid this. And yet there was a certain something about them that attracted attention, and produced results far beyond those growing out of sermons of closer thought and greater polish.

There was in them much adapted to the popular mind; they were full of plain, striking illustrations; and descriptions at times dramatic, as if he saw what he described; and, above all, full to overflowing of Bible facts and incidents.

On one occasion he took for his theme the words of Jesus to his disciples, "It is I; be not afraid." As introductory, he gave in simple, yet striking language a description of the night scene on Galilee, when the Master came walking over the troubled sea to the aid of his toiling and weary followers. Their terror, his words of cheer, the stilling of the adverse wind, and the gladness of their hearts at the sudden and needed help, were well told, and the attention of his hearers enlisted by the story of a night on the deep. He then asked, Who is this, who says, "It is I?" and answered as follows:

> *His social position was a lowly one, shown by his birth in the stable at Bethlehem, his home at Nazareth, his humble occupation, his extreme poverty, his lack of education, and having as his chief associates the poor. Moreover, he was not recognized to any great extent by the rich, had no countenance from the civil authorities, no sanction from the prevailing religion, no men of note to aid him in his enterprise; his earthly career was short; he died young. Was he nothing but what he seemed to be? Look at his wisdom! Whence came it? His power! Whence derived? What think ye of Christ? Who is this Jesus? Ask the lily, the sparrow, the sea! Ask that outstretched arm once palsied and with-*

ered! Ask that widow's son, raised by his word! Ask that judge, Pilate! Ask Death! Angels! God! Your own soul! If man only, why not another like him! Whose word so potent as his? Eighteen hundred years since he said 'Go,' and thousands now, in obedience to that command are going, to tell their fellows of his mercy and love. This Jesus gives us a command, an exhortation to courage, 'Be not afraid.' Not afraid to believe him, confess him, trust him, obey him. Be not afraid to do what he bids you—to live as he requires. Courage is needed by all; by preachers, to declare all the counsel of God; by those who are not, to faithfully discharge duty. There is too much timidity; too many fearful and unbelieving; too many spiritual doll- babies. We need soldiers, fighting men, who won't run when the devil howls. We must not be afraid to be honest, to disgorge ill-gotten gain, not be afraid to be industrious; to lay worldliness aside, to bid pride be gone! Not be afraid to work; not be too fearful to hope; not afraid to pray; not afraid to die.

"One Pearl of Great Price" was the theme of another discourse, treated in the following style:

Our Savior's discourses were adorned with gems of the mine, pearls from the ocean, or the lilies of the field; to impress his hearers with the simplicity, beauty, grandeur, and glory of his kingdom. All this preciousness of the gospel is derived from Christ, its author. The reception of Christ is the reception of his kingdom. He who possesses Christ is the owner of the most priceless pearl. Christ stands alone, superior to all earth's sovereigns. He is the 'one Lord,' 'one Mediator,' 'one altogether lovely,' 'the one Foundation,' 'the Way,' 'the Truth,' 'the Life,' 'the only name under heaven by which we can be saved.' Pearls are precious; Peter calls faith precious. Think of the preciousness of Christ, upon whom that faith reposes. Precious to the sinner, as his only Savior; precious to the Christian, as the only Mediator and High Priest; precious to the sick, as the only Physician; precious to the condemned, he only can pardon; precious to the dying, the only hope of eternal life. He will be precious to the saved, as the theme of ceaseless praise. This pearl has a price; it costs diligent search; 'Seek ye the Lord while he may be found;' 'Seek first the kingdom of God and his righteousness.' There must be a desire; we only seek that which we desire. There must be earnestness, 'Strive to enter in at the strait gate' is only another form of expression for seeking this pearl. The directions how to seek Christ are given in the gospel. Seek him by faith, by repentance, by confession; accept his offered grace in baptism. But there are those who have found where the pearl is, and will not buy, because it costs more than the mere seeking. After it was found, 'he sold all' and purchased. This selling all is not pleasant. Some do not like to give up the gratification of appetite, the pleasures of the world, their worldly companions, their sinful practices. But we must 'sell out' before we can buy this pearl. The price is not gold or silver. We may get it by sacrifice, self-denial, obedience—our wills must yield to Christ's. Finding Christ, we have all we need; teaching, pardon, peace, eternal life at last. Why, then, hoard up trash, when this goodly pearl may be yours? What honor have they who have bought this pearl! Children of God! Heirs of heaven! of joys that never end! Dear sinner, choose this priceless pearl; make not the wretched choice of eternal poverty. Give up —give up all for Christ, and make the best bargain you ever have, or ever can make."

On the "Deceitfulness of Sin," Hebrews 3:13, he indulges in the following strain:

Sin caused the fall of angels, ruined the world, robbed heaven, peopled hell. It deceives by giving false names to things; as spirit, to malice, passion, and revenge. It calls pride, true dignity; prodigality, generosity; and slander, merely openness of speech. Covetousness, is only prudence and saving; while drunkenness and reveling, are sociality. Even gambling, is either business or speculation, and a whisky-shop a saloon or coffee-house. The sinner is deceived when he pleads 'natural desire' as an excuse for evil-doing, or 'want of ability' for failing to do right; and equally so, when he claims 'others do so,' so may I. He is deceived when he makes good resolutions, only to break them, or brings up some good traits of character as an offset to his sins; deceived when he yields to temptation under the pledge to repent tomorrow, to do better by and by. Sin deceived the angels, who kept not their first estate; deceived our first parents; and will, if allowed, deceive us all. Sin hardens, as well as deceives. To God's threatenings against sin it says, 'God can't be so cruel.' It leads to rebellion against his right commands, to distrust of his promises; hardens against his providences; prosperity, calls forth no gratitude, sickness, no humility. It hardens us against the strivings of the Spirit, till the Spirit is grieved, quenched till we are lost. The remedy is to 'exhort one another.' This should be constant, 'daily,' as we are daily in danger. We should ever look to Christ's teaching and example. Let us not deceive ourselves, 'If a man seem to be religious, and bridleth not his tongue, but deceiveth his own heart, this man's religion is vain.' (James 1:26.)

Compressed within the limits of half a sheet of paper, I find the following, which is lacking in neither arrangement nor force:

"Speak unto us smooth things." (Isaiah 30:10.)

It is unaccountable that intelligent beings should become so infatuated as to prefer deceit to sincerity, falsehood to truth; and that, too, in reference to the most important of all subjects.

1. What is it to speak smooth things?

2. Why people desire it.

3. Its final results to speaker and hearer.

a. Not to be confounded with speaking kindly or affectionately. b. Nor a prudent presentation of truth, so as to avoid offense. c. Nor an appeal to candor and generosity, as Paul to Agrippa.

To speak smooth things is not necessarily to teach error, nor yet to adulterate truth. Truth may be preached in such a way that it will never save a soul; but it is, to keep back everything disagreeable to the hearers.

1st. It is to avoid a too searching process with the consciences of men. Not to offend the covetous by speaking against worldliness. Not to offend the pleasure-taker by showing its incompatibility with holy things. Not to offend the formalist by urging a spiritual religion. Not to offend the latitudinarian by declaring the woes threatened against those who preach another gospel. Not to mortify the pride of the haughty, nor assail the vanity of the ostentatious bigot. Not to arouse the careless, nor alarm the indifferent. Not to humble the spirit of the self-righteous, nor denounce hypocrisy and intemperance, nor expose the heartlessness of the selfish.

2nd. But it is to speak smooth things; to speak the truth in such a general way that none present will think that they are meant, or condemned by it.

3rd. By neglecting to enforce the threatenings of God's word, and dwelling only on the sunny side.

Balak wanted just such a prophet, to gratify his malevolence. Ahab wanted such a prophet, after killing Naboth. Herod and his unlawful wife wanted such a preacher. The Jews would never have rejected Christ, if he had preached only what they wanted to hear, and Stephen might have escaped martyrdom had he spoken smooth things. Why do people desire such preaching? Because it suits a corrupt heart and life. Because it effects an agreeable compromise with a sort of religion and their sins. The results of such preaching are: It grieves the Spirit of God; is opposed to the conduct of God's people in all ages; condemns Moses for his course toward Pharaoh; Nathan for reproving David; condemns the course of John the Baptist to Herod; Noah for warning a guilty world, and Paul for his faithful preaching to Felix. It brings ruin to the souls of preacher and people.

He used great plainness of speech, of which the following, on "The Necessity of Good Works," is an example:

Nothing should deter the minister from declaring 'the whole counsel of God.' Is 'The Righteousness of Christ' his theme? Let him set it forth, abating nothing; modifying nothing to suit the world. Let us tell the sinner what he must do to be saved; tell it all. I do not believe God could have saved the world without Christ's death. Had there been any other way, God surely would have 'spared his Son.' God applies the exact amount of power to accomplish his object; no more. He wastes nothing; there is no superfluity. Let us, then, preach the death of Christ as a necessity; heaven, hell, sin, and righteousness, as the most solemn realities. If 'good works' is our theme, we should speak out plainly; specifying the good for the encouragement of Christians, and reproving the evil with plainness; fearing no one; asking favors of no one, but 'cry aloud and spare not;' 'reprove, rebuke, exhort, with all long-suffering and doctrine.' Man is not wiser than God; we can not improve the 'first principles;' nor dare we swerve from the rest. It takes 'good works' as well as good faith, good repentance, a good confession, a good baptism, to save man, here and hereafter.

Good works occupy an important place in the divine plan; they are the evidences of our acceptance, and the proof of our love: 'If ye love me, keep my commandments.' They are not the atonement, yet they do please God, and they will receive a recompense in heaven.

There are many profitless works. There are many wicked works, which are injurious to both ourselves and our fellow men. There are works dishonoring to God; but Paul says, 'Be careful to maintain good works'. If we do these, 'we shall reap, if we faint not.' No labor done for Christ will be unrewarded. The shame we have for him is honor. Every tear, a pearl in glory's crown. The poorer we become for Christ, the richer our eternal reward, and of all the saints in heaven they shall shine brightest, and sing loudest, and enter into the fullest joy, whose lives have most resembled his. He was unselfish. He came, not to be ministered unto, but to minister. His whole life, his tears, his sorrows, his awful death, all verified his earliest saying, at twelve years old, 'I must be about my Father's business,' and because he obeyed, 'God hath highly exalted him, and given him a name that is above every name.' Hear the voice of the Spirit to John on Patmos, 'Write—Blessed are the dead that die in the Lord; they rest from their labors, and their works *do follow them.' With what feelings did Paul approach the place of execution and Stephen close his earthly career? And may we not imagine Luther, Tyndale, Wesley, Campbell, or the founder of Sunday-schools looking back upon their work, or listening to angels telling of the millions blessed by their labors. These were brilliant stars; but all may work for Christ. The mother who trains her child for God; the widow who casts in her mite to aid in any good work—all who are trying to do good; to relieve distress, to help the helpless, to heal the wounded heart, to bring a soul to Jesus, to restore a backslider, are engaged in works which shall follow them through the vale of death, and they shall not fail of their reward. Even the cup of cold water, given in the name of a disciple, shall not be forgotten in the final day. Yes, good works will be remembered and mentioned at the last day. Then shall the King say unto them on his right hand, 'Come, ye blessed of my Father, inherit the kingdom prepared for you from the foundation of the world: for I was a hungered, and ye gave me meat: I was thirsty and ye gave me drink: I was a stranger, and ye took me in: naked, and ye clothed me: I was sick, and ye visited me: I was in prison, and ye came unto me.' The value of all our works will be determined by this simple test: 'Will they follow us?' 'Will they go with us?' By our works we are to be judged, and rewarded according to them. Only what we can carry with us will be of real value to us—houses, lands, money, titles; of all these death strips us; but 'blessed are they that do his commandments.' God writes our good works in a book; a book of remembrance is kept; and though man may have forgotten, God never does. The 'faithful servant' fears not death. Should the Christian fear to die? Paul did not. No pilgrim was ever more anxious for home; no laborer for rest; no tempest-tossed mariner for*

> *the harbor; no soldier even more anxious for his crown, than was he to depart and be with Christ. See him comforting his weeping friends as they gather round him for the last time: one glimpse of Christ and heaven has taken all fear away. He speaks: I am ready—ready to be offered; welcome death; welcome the company of angels; welcome the heavenly Jerusalem. Death is swallowed up in victory; farewell. 'Be steadfast, and unmovable, always abounding in the work of the Lord, forasmuch as ye know that your labor is not in vain in the Lord.'*

On the "Triumphs of the Gospel" (2 Corinthians 2:14), he leaves the following thoughts:

> *'Thanks be to God who always causeth us to triumph in Christ.' Evidently allusion here is made to the great triumphal entries of heroes into their own chief cities after achieving great victories. Paul had his triumphs too, and breaks forth in the language of the text. Many say the gospel has done but little. Now, triumph implies conflict, and also a successful termination. By the preaching of the gospel a triumph was gained over Jewish prejudice. They had a grand system, and loved, nay, they had an idolatrous veneration for it. Abraham was the father of their nation, Moses their great lawgiver and leader, Samuel and Isaiah their prophets, David and Solomon their kings, and they looked for the Messiah to reign in splendor over them. Thousands were conquered and became the humble disciples of Christ. The gospel triumphed over various forms of Paganism. The Gentile world had its systems of philosophy, venerable and ancient, but over these the gospel triumphed. At Ephesus a great host were rescued from the false worship of Diana. In Athens, crowded with altars, the gospel gained a glorious victory. In Corinth, another great triumph. At Antioch, and even at Rome, the Church of Jesus Christ was founded by the complete triumph of the gospel; in all these places men were turned from dumb idols to serve the true God. What victories were these! No wonder that Paul exulted, and broke out in the noble words, 'Thanks be unto God who always causeth us to triumph in Christ.'*

The gospel triumphed over the corruptions of mankind, over vices horribly disgusting, and unblushingly practiced. If grand to triumph over the darkness of heathen idolatry and Jewish prejudice, it was certainly glorious to triumph over the corruptions of heart and life as did the gospel over the vileness and impurity which everywhere prevailed. The gospel made men triumph over self and the world. Those who yielded to it, had to do more than change their religion or alter their creed. They had to put the law to defiance, expose themselves to persecutions, confiscations, imprisonment, death. They had to forsake all for Christ. Yet all these trials did not hinder the triumphs of the cross. Contrast these triumphs with the victories of earth's greatest warriors—the cruel ambitious heroes with the humble apostles. Pride, lust, cruelty on one side; meekness, virtue, and good-will to man on the other. The warrior can be traced in his work of woe by footsteps of blood, the groans of the wounded, and the graves of the slain; by the desolation of the country, the sacked cities, and burning dwellings, by frenzied widows and wailing orphans, and the field of battle over which the vulture hovers or the wild beast seeks his prey.

The triumphs of the gospel are succeeded by the sunshine of peace; men are elevated, sanctified, and the blessings of heaven are brought to earth. The gospel now triumphs at home and abroad, wherever it is preached and lived faithfully. To these triumphs you owe your respectability and position in life, and woman is indebted to the gospel for her position as man's equal. To extend these victories should be the prayer and labor of all.

Sinner, let this gospel shine into your heart today, enlist and help to gain these victories, and share in the reunion on the other shore.

The above sketches are but very faint and meager outlines of some of Brother Shaw's sermons, and yet there is enough in them to correct an opinion which prevails among many who have never had the opportunity of hearing him. There is nothing in them to warrant the idea that he was light, superficial and sensational; that his sermons were chaffy, with far more human incident than gospel truth than which no judgment could be more unjust. Most of the subjects we have noticed are treated in a clear, impressive, and scriptural manner; nearly all the illustrations being drawn from the Book of God; and the impression made is that he was familiar at least with one Book, and that the best of all books for him who would teach his fellow-man the way of life and salvation. Of course the brief notes given do not do him justice, as they are the merest skeletons, which he not only clothed with flesh, but to which, by his treatment, he imparted the breath of life. They show the material with which he builded, but not the mansion he reared with them; but the colors of the artist, and the marble before it has been carved by the sculptor's hand, would come as far short of the finished picture and statue, as do these imperfect notes, of the finished sermon delivered under the inspiration of a warm heart and a crowd of interested hearers. They are but the seeds, of which the sermons growing out of them were the ripened fruit. Indeed, I feel there is nothing in the book that will give the reader a better idea of the working of his mind, and his mode of thinking, than these notes, brief and imperfect though they be.

Chapter Nine

Domestic Life—Death of His Daughter—Her Dying Words— His Dream—Musical Talent—Musical Publications—Estimate of His Musical Powers—"Bringing in the Sheaves."

Little has been said of Brother Shaw's private and domestic life. The reason of this is obvious; he belonged to the public; he lived not for himself, but for others. He was a devoted husband and a fond father, and yet so numerous and pressing were the calls for his services that he was almost constantly away from home. The short intervals between his meetings, which he was permitted to spend with his family, were highly enjoyed and greatly prized; and one of the greatest trials of his life was that of absence from those he loved.

He was the father of five children: Georgie Anna, born in Rush County, Indiana, January 3, 1856; Mary Elizabeth, born in Rush County, Indiana, October 31, 1858; John Albin, born in Rush County, Indiana, February 18, 1862; Carey W., born at Edinburgh, Indiana, February 26, 1864; and Knowles Shaw Jr., born at Lebanon, Ohio, February 14, 1869. The last two died in early infancy; the former on the 25th of July, 1865; the latter on the 13th of August, 1869; both at Lebanon, Ohio. His eldest daughter, Georgie Anna, when nearly fourteen years of age, was taken dangerously ill, while her father was engaged in a very interesting and successful meeting at Wellsburg, West Virginia. Her condition became alarming, and her father was summoned home; and a few days after his return, she calmly closed her eyes in hope and trust, on the 29th of December, 1869; to open them, doubtless, in the presence of Him to whom she had given her heart in holy obedience.

Bitter as was this trial to the father's heart, the meekness and trust of the young sufferer did much to mitigate his grief. But a short time before she breathed her last, while on the very borders of the deathless land, she exclaimed, "Look, dear father, see the angels," and, who can doubt, soon joined that company. Brother L.F. Bittle composed the following touching verses upon these her dying words, and we feel that no apology is needed for giving them to the reader:

> *Look, dear father, see the angels,*
> *As around me now they glide!*
> *They have come, I know, to guide me*
> *Thro' the Jordan's rolling tide:*
> *See you not their golden tresses,*
> *And their trailing robes of snow?*
> *Hear you not their rustling pinions,*
> *And their voices sweet and low?*
>
> *Chorus.*
> *Oh, the angels! blessed angels!*
> *Lovely as the morning star!*
> *They have come, I know, to lead me*
> *To the land that lies afar.*
>
> *I can see them bending o'er me,*
> *Feel them touch my pallid brow,*
> *As the border land I enter,*
> *And at Jordan's brink I bow.*
> *Soon they'll lead me to my Savior,*
> *Soon I'll clasp his loving hand;*
> *Then, from every care and sorrow,*
> *Safe I'll rest in Canaan's land.*
>
> *Fare you well, dear father, mother!*
> *When I reach the sinless shore,*
> *I will watch beside the river,*
> *Till the angels bring you o'er:*
> *I will be the first to greet you,*
> *When you touch the blooming strand;*
> *I will be the first to welcome,*
> *When you gain the heavenly land.*

Two of his children died in the same year; all three within about four years. These bereavements did much in drawing his thoughts upward to the dwelling-place of his dear ones, and many of his songs owe much of their tenderness and pathos to the fact that his children had become dwellers in that land of whose glories he loved to sing. No one now can read his "Lambs of the Upper Fold," or "My Beautiful Dream," without feeling that his own dear ones, safely folded in the arms of the Good Shepherd, gave the key-note to these songs. Several years after he had laid away in the grave these dear household treasures, while absent from home, holding a meeting in Louisiana, Missouri, he had a dream one night which made a deep impression upon him. He wrote it down the next morning. It was as follows:

> *"I dreamed that I slept the long night of the tomb,*
> *Then awoke from its slumber, arose from its gloom;*
> *That I wandered o'er fields in ecstatic delight,*
> *In regions of bliss where there cometh no night.*
>
> *By rivers of waters, so bright and so clear,*
> *Enchanted by music which fell on my ear;*
> *'Mid breezes that wafted its melody long*
> *While angels were singing their heavenly song:*
>
> *Where flowers were blooming that never shall die,*
> *Whose perfume was wafted by breezes on high.*
> *That land was so lovely: no sickness was there;*
> *No tears, no temptations, no sorrow, no care;*
>
> *No parting, no dying, no mourning was heard;*
> *No murmurs, complaining; there never a word*
> *That could mar the enjoyments of that happy land,*
> *Where dwelt in their beauty God's purified band.*
>
> *There we met on that shore, my dear loving wife;*
> *Yes, we met in that realm all so buoyant with life:*
> *Thy cheeks were not faded, thine eyes were not dim:*
> *There we joined in the worship and praises of Him*
>
> *Who guarded our pathway while journeying below,*
> *To crown us with blessings, all good to bestow;*
> *There songs with the ransomed thy voice joined to sing,*
> *As all shouted praises to Jesus our King.*
>
> *We wandered o'er pavements of purest of gold,*
> *By walls of rich jasper, of beauty untold;*
> *And the gates of the city were loveliest pearl,*
> *Where war's bloody banner could never unfurl.*

We talked of our journey, our joys and our woes,
As we sat where the great tree of life ever grows;
And there gathered around us our babes gone before,
And we fondly caressed them as in days of yore.

No partings were mentioned, no sorrows, no tears,
Through all the long, happy, unnumbered sweet years.
Our pilgrimage ended, at home with the blest,
For all our toils here, an eternal sweet rest.

After life's stormy voyage, a haven of peace.
After all our hard battles, a happy release;
After tears and temptations, a world of delight,
After life's bitter crosses, a crown sparkling bright,

With our children around us, though parted so long,
All singing sweet anthems of glory and song—
The sorrows of earth all over and past,
And heaven we longed for was welcomed at last.

* * *

Oh, dearest, if such be the joy of a dream,
That only can teach us of things as they seem,
What must the reality be to our souls,
As the age of bright glory eternally rolls."

This seems the most appropriate place to say something with regard to his musical powers, which on all hands are admitted to have been wonderful. No description can do him anything like justice in this respect. A power that moved multitudes, as the ocean is moved when storm-swept, and soothed hearts, when agitated, into deep tranquility, must be experienced in order to be understood; the pen is as powerless to set forth the power of his song as it would be to bring before the reader the varied play of his features, the passing shade of sadness, or the light of his smile.

He was as a singer, beyond all doubt, fully the peer of Sankey and Bliss. By many who have heard them, he was deemed superior in some respects to both. Neither ever stirred hearts more deeply than he; and we judge that the true test of the singer is to be found in the ability to move and melt the heart. Pages might be written with regard to his power over individuals and large assemblies by his singing. A single instance must suffice.

During his last meeting at Dallas, Texas, Elder Caskey, a man of great power and a natural orator, made Shaw his study, and hence, though not in a censorious, was in a critical mood; a state of mind not favorable to deep feeling or emotion. He came in to one of Shaw's morning meetings, and found him at the organ singing a song. He took a seat behind the singer, who was not aware of his presence, and soon after Shaw sang the "Old Man's Dream." Before he was half done, Caskey was weeping. The next morning Caskey was present again, and Shaw asked him to come and sit in front of him.

"No," said Caskey, "you shall not make me cry again; you opened a fountain yesterday that has been closed for twenty years. I stood over the grave of my boy once more, and saw again the wife of my youth, and you awakened memories that I thought were put away forever, and made me shed tears, a thing I have not done for twenty years before."

Reporters for the press, in the various cities in which he labored, all agreed in representing his singing as something beyond what they had ever heard before—entire audiences, filling the largest public halls, often being melted into tears. He was a perfect master of the organ. His hearers would often say, "He made it talk." He played with perfect *abandon*, bringing down his hands often upon the keys without looking at them; but there was always perfect harmony. He began to compose music soon after he began to preach; and though not entitled to rank in that respect with Bradbury and Bliss, yet there are quite a number of his compositions that would be no discredit to those great masters of sacred song. His first song was "The Shining Ones," which is still popular. He published at different times five Sunday-school singing books: 1st. "Shining Pearls." 2nd. "Golden Gate." 3rd. "Sparkling Jewels." 4th. "The Gospel Trumpet." 5th. "The Morning Star." These all met with a favorable reception—the last still meeting with a large sale.

J.H. Fillmore, whose opinion in musical matters is of deserved weight, says of Shaw: "He seemed to have an intuition as to the emotional properties of musical sounds, that enabled him to weave them together into beautiful and telling melodies. His enthusiasm in all he undertook commended it and impressed it upon the people.

With the masses, as a singer, he was a favorite; and good natural abilities, poetical and musical, with enthusiasm, tell the whole story of his success." One of his later pieces, "Bringing in the Sheaves," was dedicated to the memory of A.D. Fillmore, and has proved to be the most popular of his songs, and gives promise of living for many years to come. It was peculiarly appropriate to the memory of the sweet singer and earnest preacher of the gospel to whose name and memory he linked it, and has even a deeper significance with regard to himself. We give it below:

> *Sowing in the morning,*
> *Sowing seeds of kindness;*
> *Sowing in the noontide,*
> *And the dewy eves:*
> *Waiting for the harvest,*
> *And the time of reaping,*
> *We shall come rejoicing,*
> *Bringing in the sheaves.*
>
> *Chorus.*
> *Bringing in the golden sheaves,*
> *Bringing in the golden sheaves.*
> *Waiting for the harvest.*
> *And the time of reaping,*
> *We shall come rejoicing,*
> *Bringing in the sheaves.*
>
> *Sowing in the sunshine,*
> *Sowing in the shadows;*
> *Fearing neither clouds nor*
> *Winter's chilling breeze;*
> *By and by the harvest,*
> *And the labors ended,*
> *We shall come rejoicing,*
> *Bringing in the sheaves.*
>
> *Go, then, even weeping,*
> *Sowing for the Master,*
> *'Tho' the loss sustained*
> *Our spirit often grieves;*
> *When our weeping's over,*

He will bid us welcome,
We shall come rejoicing,
Bringing in the sheaves."

By such strains as the above he sang himself into the hearts of thousands, and in years to come the eyes of many will be dimmed with the mist of tears as they think of the sad fate of him whose songs they still sing.

Chapter Ten

Moody and Shaw Compared and Contrasted— Extracts from the Sermons of Both—Moody's Ticket and Shaw's.

A certain resemblance between Brother Shaw and the Evangelist Moody has doubtless been observed by many, and in ability to arrest and hold the attention of multitudes there was no doubt a marked similarity. At the same time, however, in respect to their teachings, there was a far more distinct and marked difference. Moody, although a Calvinist of the most pronounced New England type, always brought into prominence the more popular theories of the various religious parties, and kept out of sight the conflicting elements of the different systems. While sufficiently Calvinistic to reach those who had been brought up under such teaching, he did not carry it so far as to insist on the doctrine of particular redemption, or he never could have reached the masses, as he has done; and which must be attributed to his making the impression that the benefits of the death of Christ might be enjoyed, as they were freely offered, to all. This, of course, pleased those who accepted the doctrine of a general atonement; but it was always modified by the thought that, in order to accept the atonement, it was necessary to be made the subject of a special influence of the Holy Spirit; in this way, in effect, inserting the Calvinistic element into the Arminian view of the atonement, as in the former case he had inserted into the Calvinistic view of the atonement the Arminian element.

Carried out to its logical issue, the above method virtually denies human responsibility, by making the act of the sinner in accepting Christ to depend upon a mental and moral condition to be produced by an irresistible influence of the Holy Spirit. This was made manifest by one of his hearers, who, when asked by Moody why he had not become a Christian, replied in strict accordance with the teaching he had heard, "It has not struck me yet." It was not by a rational, intelligent conviction, but by a miraculous and irresistible power, that he supposed the change would be effected. Indeed Mr. Moody's own words are decisive upon this point. He says:

> *Let us go out and bring all our friends here, and if there is poor preaching we can bring down from heaven the necessary blessings without good preaching. In Philadelphia a skeptic came in, just out of curiosity. He wanted to see the crowd, and he hadn't more than crossed the threshold of the door before the Spirit of God met him; and I asked him if there was anything in the sermon that influenced him, in hopes that I was going to get something to encourage me; but he could not tell what the text was. I asked him if it were the singing? but he didn't know what Mr. Sankey had sung. It was the power of God alone that converted him; and that is what we want in these meetings. If we have this power, when we invite our friends here the Lord will meet them, and will answer our prayers and save them.*

A critic quite friendly to Mr. Moody says of him that "he dwells on what Christ has done in words which imply that absolutely nothing is left for man to do. In one of his addresses we find this sentence, in a paragraph whose whole tenor is to the same effect, and without qualification: *"The idea that a man can work his way up to heaven is damnable."* Mr. Moody is so absorbed in one statement of the apostles, "It is God that worketh in you," that he sometimes forgets the other clause of the same sentence, *"Work out your own salvation."* He insists, again and again, that absolutely no condition is annexed to God's offer of free pardon. There is no intimation that it is necessary to renounce and forsake sin. In one of his addresses he used the following language: "I imagine some of you will say, 'I haven't anything to do.' Well, you haven't. Salvation has been worked out for you by another." This without a word of qualification or reserve, and insisted on over, and over again. Apparently in Mr. Moody's view, Christ's sacrificial death has not only taken the place of the sinner's punishment; it has saved him from all necessity for exertion. Of the New Testament exhortation, *"Repent* and believe," Mr. Moody seems to recognize only the last half. From Genesis to Revelation he finds but one truth, free pardon through a substitutional atonement, with endless bliss or woe depending upon its acceptance by a single act of faith.

Shaw perhaps never preached a discourse without bringing

prominently forward the thought of human responsibility. One of his sermons is headed, "Hear, Believe, Do!" And while he always set forth what God, and Christ, and the Holy Spirit had to do in the work of human salvation, he never failed to show that something was needful on the part of man in order to its enjoyment, and that, not an acceptance by faith only of the offered grace, but a faith evinced by true repentance, and a yielding to, and walking in all the commandments of God.

Moody said to his hearers: "You can make yourselves Christians just about as easy as a black man can wash himself white."

Shaw said to his: "Come, for all things are now ready. The Father is ready; the Son is ready; the Spirit is ready; ministers ready; angels ready; church ready; ordinances ready. 'Christ is the author of an eternal salvation to all them that obey him.' Sinner, are you ready? When all things are ready, why not come?" And again: "It is only in obedience to the divine law that man can reap the benefits resulting from the life of love, and death sacrifice of Christ. Indeed, no man can justly claim to be reconciled to God who is not willing to yield his will and life to God; for the evidence of reconciliation is subjection to the law of God."

Moody also made the great mistake of systematically avoiding any mention of the ordinance of baptism, except to reason it away, and show its entire uselessness in the plan of salvation. In his plan it had no place, no use. He seemed to have forgotten that baptism was one of the conditions of salvation as set forth in the great commission, under which he claimed to preach; that it was everywhere enjoined by the apostles and primitive preachers, and that in their days an unbaptized convert was unknown. With them the command to be baptized was as universal as the commands to believe on the Lord Jesus Christ and to repent. Mr. Moody entirely ignored it, and in this respect was like a recruiting officer who omits one of the terms of enlistment, a physician who omits one of the essential elements of a prescription, and on the same principle that leads him to ignore baptism would deny the necessity of a ceremony to marriage, a seal to a covenant, an official name to a pardon.

His method was to soften down the harsher elements of the creed under which he had been reared; and it must be added that he also suppressed certain plain teachings of the Scriptures; that he failed utterly to "declare all the counsel of God."

In this respect, Shaw presented a striking contrast to the earnest, gifted, yet erring Moody. While insisting as earnestly as he on the necessity of faith, he also insisted on repentance toward God, and on the necessity of giving evidence of unfeigned faith, and sincere repentance by obedience to the clearly expressed will of the Master, and the uniform teaching of the apostles in regard to baptism. He taught all that Moody did in regard to faith in the Lord Jesus; and all that Moody omitted, and the Scriptures taught with regard to the ordinance, which is very generally regarded as the seal of the covenant between the returning sinner and the Savior, who accepts his submission, and freely pardons.

Moody came before his hearers claiming to be the bearer of a message from Christ to them, but kept back a part of that message, nay, claimed that a portion of the message was useless. Shaw came before his hearers with the same claim, and declared the entire message of him for whom he spake. To be convinced of this, the reader has only to consult the Acts of Apostles, and see whether the inspired preachers found in Moody, or Shaw, the most faithful imitator. To anxious, inquiring sinners, Moody never gave the same answer that was given to the same class by the apostles. Shaw never gave any other answer than that given by the apostles. Moody, unlike the apostles, never baptized his converts. Shaw, like the apostles, did invariably baptize his. The very language of the Acts of Apostles could be used without violence in regard to the results of Shaw's labors: the people "hearing believed, and were baptized." In no instance was this true of the results of the preaching of the other. In a word, Moody was a modern evangelist, using modern methods and expedients, but Shaw was an evangelist of the ancient type, telling to men in modern times the old, old story, as it was told by Peter on Pentecost, or by Paul to the Philippian jailer.

The difference between them did not consist in Moody giving the greater prominence to faith, which really was the most prominent feature of his preaching, and Shaw giving the greater prominence to baptism, which really was not the case. He insisted quite as strongly as did Moody on the absolute necessity of faith in the Lord Jesus Christ; taught that "without faith it is impossible to please God;" made it in fact an indispensable element in the salvation of the sinner; and, in addition to this, taught the indispensable necessity of repentance, making it even more prominent than Moody did, insisting that "God hath commanded all men everywhere to repent," following it up by the solemn reason that "He hath appointed a day in which he will judge the world in righteousness;" thus giving the very strongest motive to men to turn from their sins. In addition to this, he invariably taught that every penitent believer should "be baptized in the name of Jesus Christ for the remission of sins;" adding thus to the teachings of Moody an act of obedience by which faith and repentance were manifested; an act in which the names of the Father, Son, and Spirit, meet; an act in which allegiance to Satan is renounced, and allegiance to Christ pledged; an act in which submission is manifested by the sinner, and acceptance by the Savior; for in that solemn act the sinner is said to be buried with Christ and to put on Christ.

With Moody, this act had neither place nor significance in the Christian scheme. With Shaw, it was as much a part of the gospel plan, and enjoined with as much authority, as faith, repentance, or any other element of that plan, and as clearly one of the conditions of pardon as faith in the Lord Jesus Christ itself. He did not, however, attribute to it a cleansing, saving power. No one could be further from believing that water, or anything short of the blood of Christ, could cleanse the soul from sin, than he; and yet he did believe and teach that pardon was promised and bestowed on the penitent believer, when he sought it in this act of obedience, and in accordance with the teaching of the word of God. If Moody was disposed to regard baptism as useless, or at best one of the least commandments, Shaw did not so discriminate. It was enough for him to know that it was a divine command; nor did he forget that those who should break even the least of the commandments, and teach others to do so, should be esteemed least in the kingdom of heaven. Anything bearing the seal of divine authority was sacred to him. Moody said, on more than one occasion: "If baptizing a man would save him, I would do nothing else but baptize. Every man and woman I meet on the street I would persuade to be baptized. I would not wait for anything; I'd even baptize them while they were asleep, for fear that they might die before I got a chance at them."

Contrast with this the following from Shaw, on the same subject, as given by a reporter who attended one of his meetings:

> *We never heard the New Testament figure of Christ, the bridegroom, applied with greater power. He said when a young couple contracted to be married, and possessed the heart and the will for the change, all that was needed of course was the marriage ceremony to induct them into this new state or relationship to each other. That done, they are legally man and wife. They felt before precisely as they do now, only the formula of the law was wanting to permit the woman taking his name, and allowing him to claim her as his wife. So with becoming a Christian. With faith in the testimony presented comes repentance, and this produces a resolution to turn away from the past life. The change of heart is succeeded by the third step; that is, baptism into the name of the Father, the Son, and Holy Ghost. The act of baptism does not change the convert's heart—faith in the truths of the gospel did that before. It only indicates his altered condition; it is a seal to show that he has left the world and gone upon the Lord's side. Then he takes Christ's name, just as the wife takes the name of her husband when the nuptial pledge has been given. As the wife would have no authority under human law to assume the name of the husband before the marriage ceremony, so, according to the New Testament, no convert can claim the name of Christian without the final act of baptism, the line dividing the kingdom of the Devil from the kingdom of God.*

Moody seemed to regard the first item in the great commission, "He that believeth," so important as to render the rest of no value whatever; just as a man might unwisely do, who, seeing the importance of a mainspring in a watch, should so far overrate it as to regard everything else as useless; while Shaw was like a wiser man, who realized that even the mainspring was useless, unless all the other parts were in harmonious relation to it; that the absence of any part, wheel, hand, or dial, would destroy the unity and usefulness of the whole. Shaw declared the whole counsel of God. If it seem harsh, it is nevertheless true that Moody did not.

Moody's work did not contemplate the planting and training of churches. When he brought a man up to the point of saying, "I am for Christ," his work was done. No formal confession of faith in

Christ was demanded; no union with the church insisted upon. His work was as imperfect as would be that of the recruiting officer who would get men up to the point of willingness to enlist, and yet neither tell them how they from citizens became soldiers; nothing of being mustered in, of the uniform, of the armor, of the drill. When the same point was reached by Shaw it was regarded as but the initial step to a great life-work; it was the entrance upon a pilgrimage that would end but with life; a race where the crown was at the end; a warfare in which there was no rest until the last battle was fought and the victory won.

Hence, while he labored earnestly to win men to the service of Christ, he strove, with equal earnestness, to induce all such to put on the whole armor, to fight the good fight, to press forward, to lay aside every weight and the easily besetting sin, to run with patience, to be steadfast, immovable, always abounding in the work of the Lord, assuring them that their labor in the Lord would not be in vain.

The result has been that his work lives though he be dead, and gives promise of being a permanent one. The interest excited by Moody's visits, in many places, instead of developing into permanent good and steady growth, has been followed by a revulsion, anything but favorable to the cause of religion—a meteor's light, followed by intense darkness.

Under the labors of Shaw, weak churches have been strengthened, unnumbered hearts comforted; none left asking in vain, "Lord, what wilt thou have me to do?" New churches have been formed, which have grown up into strength and usefulness, and, if his works lack the meteor's splendors, they have the steady and serene light of the stars.

In zeal, energy, earnestness, in ceaseless, tireless work, there was a resemblance between the two men which few could fail to observe and admire; but, as we have shown, in their methods they could scarcely have differed more widely. Let us close the contrast with two cases.

Moody said:

> *When you go to the station and take a ticket for London, and seat yourself in the train, the guard will come and look at your ticket. He looks at that, not you. The blood is God's*

> *ticket. God says have you got your ticket, or token? If you are behind the blood you are as safe as on the golden pavement of heaven. Wake up, for you'll never get to heaven unless you are floated thither on the crimson tide of Christ's precious blood.*

Shaw said:

> *Time is short, and we have only one trip through the world, and no coming back to rectify mistakes, or make up lost opportunities; therefore do not wait to pack your trunk until the whistle blows. Have your trunk packed and a through ticket all ready before train time. Genuine tickets are stamped, "He that believeth, and is baptized, shall be saved."*

Moody's ticket fixes the attention on what Christ has done to save man, but does not show how the benefits of that death may be appropriated and enjoyed by the sinner, and is calculated to make the impression that Christ's death paid the debt, and thus set the guilty free. Shaw's ticket fixes the attention on what is necessary to be done by the sinner in order to avail himself of the benefits of Christ's death; shows that obedience is as necessary on the part of the sinner as dying on the part of the Savior; shows that Christ is "the author of an eternal salvation" (not to all men in virtue of his death), but "to all them that obey him." Moody taught that salvation was wrought out by Christ. Shaw, that while Christ died to save man, he must "work out his own salvation with fear and trembling." Moody makes everything to depend on the physician. Shaw makes the sin-sick man show his trust in the physician by taking the remedy. Moody separates faith and works. Shaw insists on their going together. Moody did not, and could not express his views in the words of Scripture. Shaw could and did express his in the very words of Christ himself. Moody, as far as we can learn, never baptized a single convert. Shaw baptized many thousands of those who heard the gospel from his lips, and were persuaded to turn from their sins to God. Which of them followed the teaching of Christ, and the example of the apostles?

Chapter Eleven

Need of Mental Photograph—A Specimen Sermon—How Readest Thou?— What Lack I Yet?

When a loved one dies, we often regret having failed to secure a picture of such a one while living; but the actual presence made us forget that the time would come when the shadow would become so dear. And so it is with regard to the addresses or sermons of those to whom in life we loved to listen. While those who give them utterance are with us, we do not think of preserving what they say, and yet what a value one of their sermons would possess when they are no longer here. Elsewhere, we have presented brief, but very imperfect, sketches of some of Brother Shaw's sermons, and we feel what a treasure it would be to have one so fully reported as to give us an idea of his treatment of his theme. He has not left such a report, nor did his friends secure one while such a thing was possible; fragments or brief sketches are numerous, but the full and complete treatment of any one of his subjects we have been unable to find. Such a report would be valuable now, not because of its intrinsic worth, but because it was *his,* and would serve to bring him up to memory as he really was.

The nearest approach to anything of this kind is in the notes of a sermon on the words, "How readest thou?" (Luke 10:26), which we give:

> *The circumstances which gave rise to the words of the text are these: A lawyer stood up and tempted Christ, saying, 'Master, what shall I do to inherit eternal life?' Christ's reply was, 'What is written in the law? How readest thou?' He is made to answer his own question by a quotation from the law, and is obliged to ask the further question, 'Who is my neighbor?' Which Christ answers by the story of the Good Samaritan, and makes the questioner again answer his own question.*
>
> *I desire to call your attention to Christ's question in three respects:*

*1st. 'How readest **thou**? as a personal matter. 2nd. 'How **readest** thou?' 3rd. '**How** readest thou?'*

The question I ask is over eighteen hundred years old. It was asked by Christ himself, hence important. I repeat it as coming from Christ, and press it home as a matter of life and death, a matter of temporal and eternal moment.

*1st. "Do you **read** the word of God at all? I ask this question, because there is no knowledge absolutely essential to man's salvation except a knowledge of things found in the Bible.*

*We live in an age when the words of the prophet Daniel are fulfilled: 'Many shall run to and fro, and knowledge shall increase.' Schools are abundant and good. Colleges and Universities of the highest type are numerous. We have books without number. More is being written, taught, and learned now than ever before in any age of the world; and yet all the education a man can get into his head could not save his soul, unless he knows and obeys the truths of the Bible. A man may be able to master half the languages of the world; he may have read books till he is a walking encyclopaedia; he may be acquainted with the stars of heaven, the birds of the air, the fish of the sea, the cedars of Lebanon; yea, he may be able to discourse upon the great secrets of earth, air, fire, and water, and still be lost for remaining ignorant of the Bible. Chemistry never silenced a guilty conscience, mathematics never healed a broken heart, philosophy can not give hope in death, natural theology gives no hope of a resurrection. All these are good and useful for earth and time, but they never did and never can raise man above earth's level. So a man may be ignorant in those things, and yet by the knowledge of that **one Book**—of one science—reach a home in heaven with God. We can get to heaven without money, health, learning, or friends, but not without the Bible.*

Then I ask again, 'How readest thou?' Because it is the book of inspiration, so unlike and superior to all others. God taught the writers what to say. When we read this Book we read God's will. This Book was written by about fifty different persons, of every rank and class of society, among them a lawgiver, a warrior king, a peaceful king, a herdsman, a Pharisee, a publican, and a poor fisherman. It was written at different times, running over a space of at least fifteen hundred years. The greater part of these writers never saw each other face to face, and yet there is perfect harmony and agreement. They all tell the same story of man the sinner, God's love, Christ's condescension and sacrifice, and the sublime plan of redemption—unfolding all man's duty and destiny. Certainly this could not be the work of chance! The Bible has been criticized, abused, burned, and blasphemed for nearly two thousand years—the busiest years of earth's history—and yet it stands, as it was given, unchanged and unimproved. The mightiest discoveries have been made, sciences have improved, customs have altered, great numbers of things once deemed useful have become obsolete, scarcely a thing but faults have been found with it, weak points discovered; but all this time the Bible has stood untouched, unchanged, perfect, because its Author is perfect. The march of intellect never overtakes it. Science develops nothing to contradict it. It meets now, as it ever has done, the wants of all ages, ranks, climates, minds, and conditions. It was 'written for our learning.' The subjects treated in the Bible are of the most important nature. It handles theories beyond the reach of man if left to himself—the soul, the world to come, eternity. How little did the wisest of the heathen know? How dim the views of Solon, Socrates, Aristotle, Plato, Seneca, and Cicero? A Sunday-school child twelve years old knows more of eternal truth than all these.

The Bible tells of the beginning of the globe on which we live; the origin of all things. It gives the only worthy account of man's origin, and the only faithful history of man. It gives true and correct views of God—that he hates sin and loves the sinner. It gives the true character of Jesus Christ—his birth, life, ministry, sayings, doings, sufferings, death, power, love, his word, his works, his thoughts, his heart. Thank God, there is one theme we can understand—Christ. The Bible contains encouraging examples of good; a rich treasury of precious promises; describes that blessed hope which is as an anchor to the soul; contains faithful warnings; our final destiny—all sealed with the precious blood of Christ.

I ask the question, 'How readest thou?' Because no book has done so much for the world. When Christ sent out his few disciples it looked like an impossibility to revolutionize the world. He sent them out when the world was full of superstition, cruelty, lust, and sin of every kind. Follow in their track and see what was done. Each man went forth then, and should now—one holy man, with one holy Book. The results, in a few years, were as follows: They pulled down idolatry, introduced a pure morality, altered the standard of purity and decency, raised the character and position of women, encountered the most cruel opposition, yet conquered, and the chains of slavery were broken by the gospel of liberty; and the glory of its victories is that they were bloodless.

This is the Book which turned Europe upside down in the days of the Reformation. It was not merely the preaching of Luther; but that which overthrew the Pope's power was the Bible, translated into German and read by the people. Not merely the quarrel between Henry VIII and the Pope, which lessened the hold of the Papacy on the English mind; it was the royal permit to have the Bible translated and placed in the churches, so that all might read it. Look at the countries where the Bible is prohibited—Italy, Spain, the South American States. Compare them with those where the Bible is free to all—England, Scotland, and the United States. We may judge of a nation by its treatment of the Bible.

To the influence of the Bible we are indebted for every humane and charitable institution in existence. The sick, the poor, the aged, and infirm; the orphan, the lunatic, the idiot, the deaf, the dumb, the blind, were seldom thought of before the Bible exerted its influence over so many lands.

Little does the scoffing infidel think, as he lies sick, far from home in some hospital, attended by kind hands, that he owes his very life to that Bible he has affected to despise. Surely such a Book as this has more than an ordinary claim upon our attention. We press, then, the question, 'How readest thou?' Read it right. It will not make you a doctor, a lawyer, an engineer, but it will make one wise unto salvation. There is another world to be thought of. The Bible can show the way to heaven. Do you read it to learn your duty? The Bible has wrought moral miracles in all ages. It has made drunkards sober; unchaste, pure; thieves, honest; violent, meek; lovers of pleasure, to be lovers of God. By it we are to be sanctified—'thoroughly furnished unto all good works.' Yes, this is one infallible guide we have, we want no other. Here infallibility resides. Not in the church, not in councils, not in ministers; it is only found in the written word of God. This is the only infallible thing on earth. If men are not benefited by it, the fault is with themselves, not the Book. Read it like the eunuch, and find Christ in it; like the Bereans, to find whether the things you have heard preached be so.

Man has awfully neglected this book. Man has a way of abusing blessings, both for the body and soul. The Catholic Church has kept, and even now keeps, the Bible from the masses. This Book, given for our learning—'the sword of the Spirit'—'able to make us wise unto salvation,' neglected! How inexcusable, O man! Seldom read but on Sunday—often not then! Read carelessly; read prayerlessly; read by scraps, with no special aim. Some neglect it because it condemns them. 'How readest thou?' By that word we shall be judged. What are other books? What are the books we read most? What are novels compared to this? We must all die, be judged, saved, or lost. Read the Bible, try modern doctrines by it, learn your duty for yourself. Read it because the good have always loved it, and found comfort in it. Read it, because it alone can give comfort in death. Worldly pleasures can not give comfort. How hollow the brilliant ball-room, the merry dance, the card-table, the

> opera, in the hour of death! Not from these, nor from those who find joy in them, do we seek for solace then. No; call one good man, with the one good Book. Let all be quiet; listen! 'Tis the voice of God; hear the sacred word! Oh how full of comfort, if a Christian, the words: 'Our light afflictions, which are but for a moment, work out for us a far more exceeding and eternal weight of glory, while we look not at the things which are seen, but at the things which are not seen; for the things which are seen are temporal, but the things which are not seen are eternal.' Oh give me my Bible and my faith, and I can bear all my trials and persecutions, and die in peace.
>
> Of all men's buried talents, none will weigh them down so heavily as a neglected Bible. As you deal with God's word, so God will deal with you. Read it with an honest purpose; read it fairly, systematically, and obey as you read, and you are safe.
>
> Men idolize their church, praise their minister, glory in their creeds, trust in their sacraments. Let us cherish the word of God. It is the lamp to our feet in life's great wilderness. It is our chart over life's stormy sea.
>
> We need Bible-reading ministers, Bible-reading congregations. Oh what blessings would follow if we were a Bible-reading nation! Sinner, turn from the world, obey the word of the Lord, and live forever.

In the delivery of the above, it was expanded to perhaps five times its present length. It is indeed only an outline, but still one that will serve to indicate the channel in which the current of his thoughts was wont to flow.

A few thoughts from a "Sermon to Young Men," will here find a fitting place. His theme was the question of the young man who came to Christ, and seemed so desirous of knowing and doing his will, who, after having said that he had kept the commandments from his youth up, asked, "What lack I yet?"

> *Religion is the most important element in character; it is the director of all the rest. Every true man, in real earnest, who*

knows what religion is, desires to become a religious man, and then to do all he can for it, and enjoy all he can of it. It does not always appear so; but it is so. They desire it with different degrees of will. We all have more or less opposition; there are many hindrances. One has a lion of a temper; another the demon of appetite—enemies within and enemies without.

Now, in this great conflict, the question by every thoughtful young man is, 'What lack I yet?' After all I have done for myself, after all that others—father, mother, friends, teachers, country, God, Christ, the Bible, the Spirit—have done, still there is a lack, what is it? Oh! 'what lack I yet?' 'One thing thou lackest.' If not a Christian you lack everything, as a corpse lacks life. Here is the sphere in which a young man can labor to gain an immortal crown, 'Seek first the kingdom of God.' Accept Christ and labor for a cause that is worthy of all your efforts. The noblest character among young men is the Christian. With what holy pride do we point to our young men who are laboring in their various professions and callings as Christians, for Christ and humanity? A host! Look at them! That young farmer, in his plain garb, who industriously toils, and honestly earns his daily bread, who leads at the same time a pious, devoted life. That young physician, who not only relieves the body of its aches and pains, but who looks to God for guidance, and has a cheerful word for his patient if a Christian, or a word of warning if a sinner; whose daily life proves him a child of God. As he sits in the great congregation, an humble worshiper with God's people, with what pleasure we point to him, thus dedicating his powers to God and humanity. Then the young Christian lawyer, who takes not a bribe against the innocent, who defends the just claim, and labors to promote law and order. With pride we point to all these and say, Behold the witnesses for Jesus. What a power for the right! What a grand company! Then the young minister, who stands as an example in word and deed to his companions and young friends; you know young men, that you love and respect him, nay, even admire him, as with tear-filled eyes he stands and earnestly pleads for souls. Oh, the honors which await such a host as this! Then let me appeal to your better judgment, and urge you to accept Christ tonight. It is just and reasonable; he demands it, and you owe it. It is the demand of gratitude; see what he has done for you. Are you not grateful for this rich offer of his love? How much happier such a course will render you. How much safer you will be—how much more useful to society and friends. You will be better sons, better brothers, better citizens, better teachers, better in any department of life in which your work may lay. God calls you, Christ died for you, the Spirit warns you, heaven opens to you, then come! Death is on your track; soon you may be among the dead. The soul requires something more than earth can give in view of death. To the Christian, death comes a welcome visitor, to deliver him from mortality, from the changing scenes and decaying body, on which time wages perpetual war, whitening our locks, furrowing our cheeks, weakening our nerves, and death comes but to deliver. Dread not then, fellow- Christian! Procrastinate not, dear sinner; come tonight; start for usefulness, happiness, and heaven."

Chapter Twelve

*Not a Eulogy, but a Life—Pen Portrait by David Walk—
Meeting at Memphis—Notices by the Memphis Press.*

"Paint me as I am," said Oliver Cromwell to the artist, who was transferring his features to the canvas, and thought to flatter him by leaving out of the picture the unsightly wart by which his face was disfigured. The stern old warrior did not wish to appear different from what he really was; he wanted his picture to be, not a flattering resemblance, but a faithful likeness, and to this, even the wart was necessary.

The biographer often falls into a similar error, when painting character; by smoothing that which is rough, or omitting that which is unsightly; but this is always a mistake, as weakness and imperfection belong to all characters, and no character is drawn to the life when these are left out. To say that Brother Shaw had no defects would be to claim more than can be claimed with truth for any mortal. The rude surroundings of his early life, his want of mental training, his lack of social culture, were all great drawbacks, and left such traces that none who knew him could fail to see. The disadvantages under which he labored were such as many a man would never have surmounted, and the wonder is, not that the rudeness, hardships, privations, and associations of early life left their indelible impress upon him; but that he was able to overcome and outgrow them to the extent he did. But even his defects were his own. They did not arise from a vain attempt to imitate the excellencies of others. They were not failures, but peculiarities, as much his own, as the outlines of his figure, the features of his face, the expression of his eyes, and the tones of his voice. Sometimes he would shock the sensitive natures of a city audience by his disregard of stereotyped proprieties, but he more than atoned for it by a tenderness and pathos which they were unable to resist; and many a preacher whose sense of propriety he violated by his rough logic and peculiar mannerisms, would gladly have exchanged his own purer style and more refined manner for Shaw's wonderful power over the minds and hearts of men.

There were times when his tall, angular, and somewhat ungainly figure, assumed an air of majesty, and the message he delivered lost nothing by the appearance and manner of the messenger; for self was forgotten, and the message engrossed all his thoughts. He looked and spake, as we may imagine the prophets and apostles did when they rebuked the people of Israel for their sins, or entreated lost sinners to be reconciled to God. His deep, unfeigned earnestness rendered his hearers unmindful of any defects in manner, and his evident sincerity disarmed criticism. Dead though he be, we desire the reader to see him as when living, and shall present him as he appeared to his most impartial critics, ere death had turned all criticism into tenderness, and eyes that might have been keen to observe defects were dimmed with tears. The following sketch is from the pen of David Walk, in the winter of 1877:

> *I first met Brother Shaw in Edinburgh, Indiana, January 3rd, 1863. He was devoting a portion of his time to the church in that town, and I think a portion to the church called New Hope, in the country, a few miles south of the former place. At all events, after the close of my meeting at Edinburgh, he was with me in a meeting at New Hope, and subsequently at Columbus, the county seat of Bartholomew County, still south of New Hope.*
>
> *The first impression made upon me by Brother Shaw was **unique**. He did not strike me as possessing any of the commonly-accepted and conventional characteristics of a preacher; tall, raw-boned, angular, and awkward, he gave no promise then of the wonderful career he afterward accomplished. He seemed to me to be a "Jack of all trades." He was agent for a sewing machine, and much of his time was spent in this behalf. In our walks around the town and country he would unceremoniously dodge into a house, sit down at the machine, adjust it, and then sew for dear life on whatever garment was in hand. Oftener than otherwise, it would be some article of a lady's clothing. All this he did with the utmost coolness, and apparently unconscious of anything unusual in his conduct. He was very fond of playing the violin, and often, after the services, would spend*

an hour or two in this not unpleasant diversion. He was all unschooled in the conventionalities of polite society. One rainy afternoon, at New Hope, a number of candidates were to be baptized. As I did all the preaching, he proffered his service as baptist. We repaired to a beautiful stream in the near neighborhood, where the ordinance was administered. Returning to the house of our host, he refused to make any change in his clothing, but stood and sat around the fire-place all the afternoon, in his bare feet, drying his clothes, regardless of all around. This was quite shocking to my notions of decorum, but he seemed to make no account of the circumstance. In some respects, he seemed to me to be as simple and unaffected as a little child, and in others, to be entirely self-conscious. He thought that what he did was all right, and better than any one else could have done it. He affected, even at this early date, considerable literary skill, and did not hesitate to correct my grammar, rhetoric, and logic. He even undertook to show me how to preach, and succeeded more to his own satisfaction than to mine.

After this, I met him occasionally at our general Conventions, at Cincinnati and elsewhere, but had no special or personal knowledge of him for many years. Notes of his peculiar fame, and the reputation he was making in the field, from time to time reached me. All that I heard and read concerning him caused me to wonder greatly, remembering, as I did, his unpropitious beginning. After I had been preaching at Memphis some seven or eight years, the brethren, with my approval, determined to give him a trial in that eminently conservative, and socially and religiously moss-grown city. Soon after his meeting closed I prepared the following notice of it for the Christian Standard, which will sufficiently set forth the character and results of his first effort there:

KNOWLES SHAW IN MEMPHIS.

M<small>EMPHIS</small>, *March 7, 1877.*

Dear Brother Errett:—*I did not intend to say much about our late meeting in this city; for, apart from other reasons, you have already published a lengthy and very just notice from one of our daily papers. But from all quarters the cry comes: "Tell us about your meeting." "How did Brother Shaw take in Memphis?" "What do you think of his work?" etc., etc. From all of which I am led to understand, there is a general and widespread desire for some information beyond a mere statement of the facts and results of the effort. I shall endeavor, therefore, to give an honest and faithful report of the preacher, his methods, and the results — as they appear to us here on the ground.*

In the first place, I may say that we were agreeably disappointed in every way. With us it was an experiment. We had heard so much of Brother Shaw's eccentricities that it was with sober misgivings we finally concluded to invite his aid. He came unheralded. No one outside of our church had so much as heard of him. He at once took the community captive. No man ever before created so profound an interest among all classes. Soon our large house was filled to its utmost capacity, while hundreds were turned away for want of room. And he held this audience steadily to the end. Many of the ministers of the city put in an appearance—some of them very often—and expressed their hearty sympathy with the work, and were earnest in prayer, and expressions of good will, until Brother Shaw included obedience as a part of the gospel; then they dropped him. I shall always honor Brother Shaw for his fidelity to the whole, round gospel of Jesus Christ. Amid the greatest temptations to concede, to modify, to tone down something of the truth, he stood like a wall of fire in defense of the whole truth. No man was ever more faithful to the gospel. I want this fact to be distinctly noted. He could have carried the whole city, and every church and preacher in it, had he consented to stop where Moody, Whittle, and other celebrated revivalists stopped; but no: he preached the gospel as it was preached by those who were first divinely commissioned to preach it by the anointing of the Holy Spirit. There might be a thousand objectionable things in Brother Shaw's methods, but this one fact would make me overlook them all. But is there anything objectionable? Well, that is largely a matter of taste. I have yet to hear and see the man who in all respects is unobjectionable according to my ideas of taste and propriety. I suppose there are some who would object even to—me! He has some oddities, some idiosyncrasies, but they are so obviously natural to the man as not to appear very incongruous or inharmonious. I rather like them. I would not like to see Brother Errett, or Brother Pendleton, or Brother Lamar, undertake the same pulpit, philological, and rhetorical feats; but I see no impropriety in Brother Shaw attempting them, for he succeeds in them; whereas, the brethren above mentioned would make sorry work of it. For example: Imagine Brother Pendleton leaving the pulpit in the midst of his sermon, and, going to the remotest corner of the house, mounting a bench, and singing with most lugubrious air and whine—

How tedious and tasteless the hours,

in illustration of the half-hearted, back-slidden Christian, who needs a protracted meeting every six months in order to keep any life in him.

But when the protracted meeting has well advanced, this same remote-corner-Christian rushes to the front, singing with great vim—

Am I a soldier of the cross?

just as Brother Shaw did, suiting the action to the word. Well, this is precisely what he did, and what is more, he did it successfully.

Of course, his ability to sing adds greatly to his power, and is a large element to his success in attracting and holding great audiences. He is as good a singer as either Sankey or the lamented Bliss, an infinitely better preacher than either Moody or Whittle. There! I have done it. But if anybody can show to the contrary, let him do it.

I do not mean to be understood as approving all Brother Shaw does and says. Far from it. I would not like him as a regular diet all the year round. He would be none the less useful and powerful were he to leave off some things, while at the same time he would conciliate hypercritical enemies of our cause. I told him this eight or ten times, but I do not think he heard me. He is too much absorbed in his work, and himself, to listen to the suggestions of age and wisdom. He has, I observe, a very fine opinion of Knowles Shaw. He will read these strictures, laugh at them, and the first time he meets me slap me on the shoulder and say: "Walk, that was a good thing. Ha, ha, ha!" And that will be the end of it. He will die thinking it a good joke, and never will believe that I am in solemn earnest.

He repeats himself too much. Many of his most effective sermons are marred by personal allusions, which, often repeated, lose their original force. Twenty-seven times he referred to the fact that he had made five funeral marches to the grave from his broken and desolated home. The first time he told this, it took the house by storm. Sixty-nine times he stated that in early life he fiddled for balls, parties, and theaters. He intended to illustrate the point that he was a great sinner saved by grace. Well, for the first forty or fifty times this fact of his youthful history had considerable power, but after that it became monotonous. But he can not be judged by any ordinary rule. Perhaps if he were to leave off the things of which I complain, he would be shorn of his power, and become altogether like the rest of us—weary, respectable plodders, who utterly fail, with all our refinement and elegance, to stir the public heart.

To show my sincerity, I will say that, if it were God's will, I would be glad to exchange my gifts for his. But it does appear to me that if I could sing as he can, and preach as he can, I would not need some of the accessories which he deems indispensable.

What was the outcome of all this? Well, hundreds of people heard the gospel who never heard it before. And an interest was created in behalf of the cause in this city that never existed before.

We love Brother Shaw so much that we are determined to

> *have him again. We have actually engaged him for another meeting, and the time is set, but for prudential reasons we want nothing said about the time.*
>
> *We are going to make one more effort to win men to Christ. We need and we ask the prayers of the whole brotherhood. Brethren, pray that God will give us the victory in this wicked city.*
>
> *David Walk.*

To many, the above may seem *severely* just, but it has the merit of being a faithful picture, which those who knew Brother Shaw best will not be slow to recognize. He said of it himself that it was the best, most appreciative, just notice, that had ever been written of him. Brother Walk adds: "He was my guest five weeks, slept every night in my house, and ate nearly every meal at my table, and whatever criticisms either I or any member of the family had to make concerning his peculiarities, all were agreed in the judgment often expressed: 'Brother Shaw is a *good* man.' "

Brother Shaw's own brief report of the above meeting is as follows:

> *I held a meeting of near three weeks with the Linden Street Church in Memphis, Tennessee, of which Brother Walk has been the faithful and successful pastor for over eight years, which closed on the 14th inst. There were twenty-eight confessions, and during the entire meeting the house, which has capacity to seat seven hundred, was filled, and sometimes hundreds had to go away. Brother Walk is the best manager of a church I have found in my rounds. Backed by a good, intelligent, and zealous board of elders and deacons, success is not wonderful. I have received a call to return and hold a two weeks' meeting before long, as we could hardly call the other work finished.*

The Memphis papers speak of Brother Shaw's work with warm and unqualified approval, as the following extracts show:

THE SINGING EVANGELIST.

> *Our religious reporter was in attendance at the Linden Street Christian Church both morning and night on Sunday*

last. He had heard much of the marvelous revivalist now conducting services in that sanctuary; and he concluded to see and hear for himself, and then to favor the public with his views of the situation. Mr. Shaw is a tall, rawboned, rather ungainly specimen of the genus homo, standing about six feet four inches in his boots. His hair and beard are very luxuriant as to quantity, and dark auburn as to color. His articulation, while unusually rapid, is at the same time wonderfully distinct. In style and manners he defies all known and unknown rules. He is emphatically a law unto himself. He gets right down to business without wasting any time in prosy preliminaries. The first sentence is of as much consequence, and likely to be as sharp, as any that follows. He is intensely in earnest. He evidently believes the message which he brings to others. It absorbs and controls every faculty of his mind, and exercises every muscle of his body. He is very plain and practical. A little child can easily follow him. We judge that he lays no claim whatever to being a chaste and finished orator, for such he certainly is not; but it must be confessed that he wields a strange power over his audience —one moment the face is wreathed in smiles, the next the eyes are overflowing with tears.

As to his ability as a singer we have heard a variety of opinions expressed by those competent to judge, the average opinion being that he is about the equal of the late Mr. Bliss. It is agreed that in the low notes Mr. Bliss was his superior, but in the highest register, and in strength, volume, and sweetness, Mr. Shaw is greatly the superior of the lamented Bliss. This, of course, gives him an immense advantage over the mere preacher, for long before he has announced his subject, he has sung his audience into deep and earnest sympathy with himself. But our readers must go and judge for themselves. No brief notice, such as we are able to give, will do justice to this really extraordinary man. They will see and hear some things which they will doubtless not approve; but, on the other hand, they can not but be benefited by the pure, and wholesome teachings of the evangelist. The audiences were immense on both occasions, and the capacity of the house is likely to be taxed more than it can pay. We suggest to the deacons, Greenlaw Opera-house. Give the masses a chance.

The progress of the meeting was noticed as below:

The work of evangelism, under the conduct of Knowles Shaw, still continues at the Linden Street Church. On Sunday night the audience exceeded nine hundred persons, one-third of whom stood during the long services, and as many turned away because of lack of comfortable accommodations. The preacher took for his subject, 'Decision of Character,' addressing himself particularly to young men and women. He delineated with unerring certainty, with the skill of a deft limner, the characteristics essential to the perfection of manly or womanly virtue, and to their value as influential entities in the social, moral and religious sphere. Mr. Shaw seized hold of Daniel and Esther, of Scripture, as models of decision of character, pointing out what in them evoked their useful and influential development. This lecture was listened to with seeming interest by the congregation, among which our reporter counted ten lawyers, two judges, eight doctors of medicine, and six ministers of the gospel. The services of last evening were also largely attended, the theme of the sermon being, 'Almost Persuaded.' Upon this occasion some half-dozen persons were added to the church by open confession. We understand that the meetings will continue during the succeeding nights of the week, the subject for this evening being, 'Honoring God.'

***

The revival services, conducted by Mr. Shaw, at the Linden Street Christian Church, were again largely attended last night. The house was crowded to its utmost capacity. Many persons stood during the exercises, while others, not being accommodated with seats, went away. Mr. Shaw, selecting a text from Amos, one of the minor prophets, the fourth chapter and twelfth verse, warned the people to 'Prepare and meet their God.' The discourse was well balanced between the individual experiences and observations of the speaker and the way of the preparation which every man should adopt in order to meet the great 'Judge of the quick and the dead.' The sermon was strongly doctrinal, involving in its development the tenets or principles of the church represented by the evangelist. He defined with frankness, fullness, and clearness his views in reference to the purposes of baptism, without in any way alluding to, or discussing the modes of administration of this solemn ordinance. He stated that he dwelt particularly upon the subject of a preparation because of the fact that his people (the Campbellites) had been misunderstood as to the intent and purposes of baptism under their practices. The attention of the congregation was marked by courtesy, and if the vanity of the preacher can be excited by the crowd and interest manifested, then the evangelist should be satisfied. Some additions were made to the church at the close of the exercises.

***

Mr. Shaw held forth last night at the Linden Street Christian Church to a crowded house, the subject of his discourse having been, 'Heavenly Recognition.' The speaker presented the subject clearly, although the discourse was less replete than any preceding one with scriptural citations. He handled the matter most interestingly, and, at times, spoke with deep feeling and touching pathos. His sermon consumed one hour and five minutes, but the audience manifested no impatience, nor disposition to retire before the conclusion. On the other hand, a large body of the congregation lingered after the closing to talk with Mr. Shaw, and with one another. He announced that since beginning the services of the evening, he had been handed a copy of the last song ever composed by his friend and late singing companion, Mr. P.P. Bliss, and though entirely new to himself, he would sing the same this evening. That, as this sweet singer in Israel was held in such affectionate remembrance by the people of Memphis, and everything connected with his life and death would be so gladly re-

ceived by them; at the close of tonight's services, he would give to the audience some facts, both of the work of Mr. Bliss, and also everything that had been discovered in reference to the last moments of the lamented man and wife, and the memorial services after their death. The subject of Mr. Shaw's discourse, tonight, will be: 'The fullness of the times, or the great consummation.' It is probable that the labors of the evangelist in this field will then close, as he has engagements elsewhere.

From the above we gather that the interest was great, but by no means unusual. Even greater interest, and much greater success, had attended his labors at St. Louis, Covington, South Bend, and many other places, before that visit; and not long after New Orleans was visited, and did not prove an exception to the rule.

We can not close this chapter without calling attention to the fact, that Brother Walk's first impressions with regard to Shaw were received, when the latter had been but a short time before the public, and these may have had more influence than he was aware of in regard to the views expressed in the latter part of his article. We think it therefore eminently proper to give the views of other competent judges with regard to him when he had outgrown much that Brother Walk noted in the early part of his career, which we shall do in the next chapter.

Chapter Thirteen

The Editor of the Christian Preacher on Shaw's Method and Manner—Elder Caskey's Review of Wilmeth, and Opinion of Shaw—The Editor's Rejoinder.

It is quite likely that Brother Shaw never had fuller and freer command of his powers than during the meeting at Memphis, which is described at length in the preceding chapter. He was then forty-three years of age, mature in body and mind, and as full of purpose as ever to spend the remainder of his life in his chosen work. In the next year, which none who knew him thought would be his last, before his vigor had departed or any of his powers had suffered a sad eclipse, he labored with wonted zeal and with great success; and during his last meeting at Dallas, Texas, he was described as follows by two different writers, who never had met him till then. The first was [C.M. Wilmeth] the editor of the *Christian Preacher,* published at Dallas, Texas, who thus sketched him in the columns of his paper:

> *Knowles Shaw, as a revivalist and musician, has a national name. He is tall and well proportioned, has a searching eye, a cheerful countenance and luxuriant whiskers, and is past the meridian of life.*
>
> *He has preached about nineteen years; in almost all the States of the Union; and has baptized over eleven thousand. He is the author of a number of music-books; sings in several languages; and plays on many kinds of instruments. He reasons like Paul; is as bold as Peter; and as tender as John. He is natural like Shakespeare; witty like Swift; and pathetic like Burns. He is as independent as Beecher; as idiosyncratic as Talmage; and as indefatigable as Moody. He sings with the energy of Sankey; and plays with the action of Blind Tom. He can support the character, in the same scene, of clergyman and clown, actor and ape, nightingale and parrot. During his discourse, you may see him pacing the platform singing some thrilling song of Zi-*

> on, or seated by the organ playing some touching sentimental ballad. You may behold him on bended knee, before some cruel king, in tender tones imploring mercy; or perched upon the end of a bench, off in the amen corner, stiff as a poker and cold as a midnight spook, burlesquing the lukewarm Christian to the tune of
>
> > How tedious and tasteless the hours.
>
> You may behold the audience baptized in tears, while he stands in memory by the bed-side of a beautiful dying daughter, who says, 'I'm going home, dear father, and after a few more years of toil and tears you'll follow me;' or you may see them convulsed with laughter, as he portrays, in pantomime, with walled eyes and distorted countenance, gestures and grips, grimaces and grins, a balky horse or a bad boy.

The second article shows that the first impression was strengthened by his subsequent efforts:

> Brother Shaw has been with us a month, and has added more than a hundred to the Commerce Street congregation. At other places, he has added, in the course of a single meeting, several hundred. During a ministry of twenty years, he has averaged over five hundred additions a year. Besides these 'visible results' of his preaching, of course the good seed is sown in many other hearts, and the church is generally strengthened in its faith and zeal. These extraordinary results make us inquire, What are the secrets of his success? It has been suggested by some of the Baptists that they create a chair in their Theological Seminary to teach how to hold revivals; and one of their editors mentions Major Penn as a suitable professor to fill that chair. Certainly Knowles Shaw would make a better Professor of Revivals than Major Penn; and, as he can not take the time from evangelizing to formally fill a collegiate chair, we propose, in lieu of that, to gather up for our readers some of the golden filings that fall from his evangelistic machinery. First, he wins the people's ears before he woos their hearts. His reputation gives him the vantage ground in this. But a

reputation can not hold a congregation after a first hearing, if a reputation is all the speaker possesses. He says that if he were called upon to give the three elements of success, he would say, 'First, work; second, <u>WORK</u>; third, WORK.' So he works from the commencement of a meeting to its close—all over and in every way. He sometimes sees to the proper ventilation of the room, and to the seating of the audience. He plays the instrument and leads the music. He reads the Scripture, and comments and illustrates as he reads. He does some of the praying and all of the preaching. If another baptizes, he directs and assists actively all the time. With all the assistance that a live congregation can give, yet there is as great a proportion of Shaw in one of his meetings as there is water on the world. While something may be lost by not having others to labor, this very individuality always attracts the people; and, being a 'master of assemblies,' he leads them along, step by step, without offense. Secondly, he utilizes music to its utmost. Not only does he train the audience rigidly upon new songs, and the proper rendition of the more familiar; but occasionally he sandwiches into the rehearsal a solo, or into the sermon a sentimental, thereby stirring the emotions from their very depths. Although his voice is somewhat impaired by protracted preaching, yet he sings with such remarkable clearness and precision that it greatly compensates for the lack of volume and tone. The chief charm of his singing is his invariably distinct enunciation. Every word is distinctly heard, though it be a whisper. His music bears the precious truth straight to the heart. If he seems to unscientifically snap off a strain, it is simply to put a cracker on it which will be felt. Though we have heard finer vocalists, we scarcely have met a man who could so successfully sing his sentiments into the souls of the people. Thirdly, his preaching is attractive, instructive, and powerful. He has much of 'the milk of human kindness' in his heart; so that his sermons abound in touching illustrations from experience and observation. The hand of affliction has been laid heavily upon him, having buried out of his sight in one year five of his family; and, knowing the sorrows of this life, he *can persuade men to prepare for a better. He depends largely upon the power of God's word. He does not trust to his singing, his prayers, and his illustrations, but to the incorruptible seed to enliven the sinner. His preaching is equally divided between saint and sinner, and he is as pointed to the saint as the sinner. His scathing of sin in professed Christians can not be too highly commended, while it is all done in a kind spirit and an inoffensive style. His language is generally beyond criticism, and is often very elegant, though sometimes tinctured with uncanonized words. He is not pedantic, makes no pretensions to profundity; being rather desirous of making things plain and pointed. Finally, he is true to one of his mottoes, 'Much go-ahead- itiveness and never-let-go-itiveness.' He continues a meeting till it is concluded, and only concludes it when he concluded there are no others to be reached by it. This is an improvement upon what is common in our country. We surrender the field as soon as we have thrown up a few entrenchments. We sow a few seeds, generally, and leave them to germinate and die without watering or cultivation. He sometimes remains with a congregation for a year after an ingathering, which, in entirely new congregations, we deem eminently necessary and scriptural.*

Much is yet to be learned by us about planting the gospel; and it is hoped that the above may help us on to some better knowledge of preaching the truth. While in every man we may find faults, we do not wish to copy; we should ever be ready to separate the golden wheat from the worthless chaff, and appropriate it for good. It would be gross presumption to say that we could learn nothing from Knowles Shaw, who has stirred Dallas to its depths.

Some expressions in the foregoing were regarded as ill-chosen, and called forth the following from Elder T.W. Caskey, well known through the South as one of the ablest preachers in the State:

CASKEY ON SHAW.

Sherman, Texas, May 18, 1878.

Brother Mac:—*Some of Brother Shaw's friends are somewhat grieved at your pen-portrait of the man, but I think they are more sensitive than need be, for you attribute to him the leading and best element of many of the greatest names that have brightened the pages of sacred or profane history: Paul, Peter, John, Shakespeare, Swift, Burns, Beecher, Moody, Talmage, Sankey, and last, but not least in his line, Blind Tom, the greatest musical genius of the world. The man who possesses these, certainly stands upon the head of the highest of his fellows. Give me but half of these, and I'll agree to pack the whole spotted breeches family, the whole monkey tribe, the parrot and all other discordant-noted birds, together with Blind Tom and the whole African race thrown in. The versatility of genius ascribed to him is simply wonderful, not more so than true.*

If any injustice is done to Brother Shaw, it is in the latter part of your article, where you use the terms latitudinarianism, preaching through envy, etc. If you intend this to to apply to Brother Shaw, you have done him great injustice, and I know you will make the amende honorable; for doctrinally, as far as I have heard him, he is as narrow- gauged as Brother Benj. Franklin would have him to be. As to his eccentricities, they are God-given and not assumed, and to accomplish one-half as much as he does I would agree to shoulder them all and as many more. Brother Shaw says and does many things I could not do if I would, and would not if I could, and which, of course, I do not approve; but this is not the trouble with me. My trouble is T.W. Caskey does the same, and I certainly don't want him to come to my standard.

If Brother Shaw preaches Christ through envy, then my prayer to God is, to greatly increase his envy; if the Commerce Street Church is having it done through envy, and are working as they have been and are, then may a Pentecostal shower of it fall upon all the churches in Texas.

T.W. Caskey.

This called forth the following explanation:

In our article, alluded to above, some things were said which no doubt jarred upon the ears of some persons. On the contrary, however, it struck a vein of approval and applause in the hearts of a host of brethren.

The comparison to Blind Tom was not made because he is a negro, but because he is a musical genius, well known and universally admired. [Note: the author of this piece was also black] *The point of comparison was not as to color, sense, or profession, but as to 'action.' It is sometimes said of those who can not refrain from dancing when they hear music, that their music is located in their feet; but Brother Shaw's is located all over him. His body sways to and fro, like a tall pine in a storm; his head bobs up and down and about, his long beard following like the train of a comet; his face is now bowed horizontal with the floor and then upturned to the ceiling; his eyes turning by times to all points of the compass; and his left hand has a peculiar crow-hop from the key-board of the organ over his head, there hanging, while he dwells on a long note. This is Knowles Shaw, and it reminds us of Blind Tom's action at the piano, and his after clapping of hands. As to the expressions 'clown,' 'ape,' 'parrot,' etc., they were simply the most suitable words by which to give forcible expression to the facts in the case.*

We did not accuse Brother Shaw of latitudinarianism, but of the 'semblance of latitudinarianism.' In the earlier part of his meeting he spoke of his preaching having resulted in some places in adding members to the Baptist and Methodist Churches as well as to his own; used the term 'Campbellism' in such a way that opposers quoted him as sanctioning its use; and now and then ridiculed such principles as, 'Where the Bible speaks, we speak; and where the Bible is silent, we are silent.' Be it said to his praise, however, that the inferences drawn from such slipshod expressions have been chiefly dispelled by plain and pointed discourses, upon first principles and lucid and touching lectures upon Christian duty. He fights carnality and uncleanness with all the vim that's in him. He even gave

Brother Caskey some sharp raps on the knuckles for chewing his quid and squirting his tobacco juice. The dance and the dram-shop receive no mercy from his hands; and right well did we enjoy his thunderbolts against them. He can beat the man that makes them, telling temperance anecdotes.

No man of ordinary abilities could have called forth such unstinted praise as this from strangers; and one of them, Elder Caskey, says that before hearing him he had been somewhat prejudiced against him by the reports he had heard with regard to his eccentricities and peculiarities. Not only was this prejudice removed by what he saw and heard, but he declared, "Such a man I never met before on life's journey, and never expect to meet again till its journey ends."

But, apart from all that has been said of him, we have twenty years of such faithful and earnest work as the world has seldom seen; and this will give the best idea of the man, and it is hoped will lead others to a noble emulation of his labors.

Chapter Fourteen

Extent and Variety of His Labors—Extracts from Diary for 1877— Last Day at Home.

To give an idea of the variety and extent of Brother Shaw's labors, it has occurred to me that the best way to accomplish this would be to review the work of an entire year. For this purpose I have chosen the year 1877; not because it was one of his most laborious and successful ones, but because it is the only one of which I have a full and connected record. The first day of the year found him at Columbus, Mississippi, and the first lines in his diary are:

> *Lord, help me this year to do more for thee than in any previous year in winning souls to Christ. Convinced of my weakness and asking his strength I commence the work.*

His first day's work shows that he was instant in season and out of season. The record is brief:

> *Monday, January 1, 1877. Deep snow. At 10 A.M., two men and two boys present. Read psalm, prayed, and sang. 7 P.M., Subject, 'Watchfulness.' Twenty-five persons out; and some feeling.*
>
> *Tuesday, 2nd, 10 A.M. Twelve persons out. Subject of discourse, 'Nearness to the Cross.' 7 P.M. Subject, 'Mercy and Obedience.' Better audience. Fifty persons out; good attention.*
>
> *Wednesday, 3rd, 10 A.M. Subject, 'Christian Usefulness.' Twenty-one present; good interest. 7 P.M. Subject, 'Witness of the Spirit.' Seventy-five present, among them Baptist and Presbyterian ministers.*
>
> *Thursday, 4th, 10 A.M. Subject, 'Prayer.' Thirty- six present; good impression and feeling. Praise God. 7 P.M. Subject, 'Glorious Gospel.' One hundred present; remarkable attention. Praise God.*

Friday, 5th, 10 A.M. Subject, 'Patience.' Fifty-four present. 7 P.M. Subject, 'Resisting the Spirit.' Good crowd. Thank God.

Saturday, 6th, 10 A.M. Subject, 'Believe, Love, and Do.' Sixty out—two preachers; good impression. Lord, give us a good work tonight. 7 P.M. Subject, 'The Faithful Saying.' Good audience.

Sunday, 7th, 10 1/2 A.M. Subject, 'God the Just and Justifier.' Fine audience. Blessed meeting. 3 P.M. Subject, 'Who is on the Lord's Side.' House full. Praise God. 7 P.M. Subject, 'Decision.' House crowded.

Monday, 8th, 10 A.M. Subject, 'Christian Progression.' Fifty present. 7 P.M. Subject, 'Prepare to Meet thy God.' Three came forward; two confessed Christ.

Tuesday, 9th, 10 A.M. Subject, 'Prerogatives.' Eighty present; one confession. 7 P.M. Subject, 'Almost.' House filled; three confessions.

Wednesday, 10th, 10 A.M. Subject 'Harvest.' 7 P.M. Subject, 'Church and Preparatives.' Good audience; fine attention. Lord, grant us fruit for Jesus' sake.

Thursday, 11th, 10 A.M. Subject, 'All Sufficiency in Christ.' Good audience and attention. 7 P.M. Subject, 'What Must I Do?' Lord help us, forgive us, save us, and bring others to thy Cross.

Friday, 12th, 10 A.M. Subject, 'Christ's Temptation.' 7. P.M. Subject, 'Honoring God.'

Saturday, 13th, 10 A.M. Subject, 'The Lord's Side.' 7 P.M. Subject, 'Pilgrim's Invitation.'

Sunday, 14th, 10 1/2 A.M. Subject, 'Mediation.' 7 P.M. Subject, 'Witness of the Spirit.' House crowded to overflowing.

Monday, 15th, 10 A.M. Lecture. 7 P.M. Subject, 'Christ Justified.'

Tuesday, 16th, 10 A.M. Subject, 'Evil Communications.' 7

> P.M. Subject, 'Sanctification.' House filled.
>
> Wednesday, 17th, 10 A.M. Subject, 'Morning Star.' 7 P.M. Subject, 'God's Righteousness.'
>
> Thursday, 18th, 7 P.M. Subject, 'Angels.' House filled.
>
> Friday, 19th. Started for Memphis. O Lord, may our Memphis work be a glorious one for Jesus' sake!"

At Memphis he remained nearly three weeks, creating great interest, and gaining about thirty additions. The particulars of this meeting are given elsewhere, in the admirable sketch by Elder D. Walk, who was pastor of the church at Memphis at that time. After a brief sojourn at home, during which he preached almost daily, he went to Paducah, Kentucky, on the 22nd of February, and at once gained a large and attentive hearing, which continued to the close. He was there some twelve days, and had twenty-five additions.

At a previous meeting, at the same place, fifty-four were added. Geo. E. Flower, who was pastor of the church there at that time, writes on February 11th, 1879: "No man ever visited Paducah that did as much good as Brother Shaw. It has sometimes been said that the members he took in were stony-ground hearers. It was not the case with us; they are most of them faithful yet."

After a three weeks' sojourn at home, not to rest, but labor, he started, on the 28th of March, for New Orleans; and immediately on his arrival entered on his work. He soon perceived that the field was an extremely difficult one in which to labor, and would require more time to work up an interest than his other engagements would allow. Under these circumstances he thought it best not to make the attempt. He was persuaded to remain, and went to work, if possible, with more than his wonted zeal and earnestness; had hand-bills struck, and went to the Mayor of the city to obtain permission to preach in Lafayette Square on Sunday afternoon. The Mayor at first refused permission, but afterward granted it; and on Sunday afternoon he held an outdoor service in the Public Square above mentioned. This advertised his meetings at the church and the house was soon filled. Soon it became necessary to fill the aisles with chairs; then every foot of standing-room was occupied, and many were unable to find even an entrance. By the next Sunday his meeting was well advertised, and on the afternoon of that day he addressed an audience of some two thousand persons: among them beggars, tramps, roughs, boot-blacks, and newsboys; many of whom had never heard a sermon before, and who would not have heard that if they had been obliged to enter a church to do so. On the next Sunday the crowd in the Square was still larger, and his meetings were regarded as a complete success. He made several temperance speeches while there, which were well received, and few men ever made themselves more widely or favorably known in New Orleans, within the space of less than three weeks, than did Knowles Shaw. Eleven persons were added to the church during this visit, and impressions were made on others that will never be forgotten.

The following notice is from the New Orleans *Times:*

THE SINGING EVANGELIST.

Hearing much of Rev. Knowles Shaw, the celebrated singing evangelist, now visiting this city, our reporter concluded last night to see and hear for himself, and hence was in place 'on time' at the Christian Church, corner of Camp and Melpomene Streets. At 7:15 Mr. Shaw came in with hasty step and seated himself at the organ in front of the congregation and promptly began the 'thirty-minutes service of song,' which precedes each sermon. It was manifest in a moment that he was master of the situation—that he understood his work and meant to execute it promptly. His business-like management of affairs was the first noticeable peculiarity. 'The service of song' was interspersed with solos, in which the evangelist, though a little hoarse from cold, evinced wonderful power. This part of the service the large audience present seemed to enjoy very much.

Following this was the sermon, in which the speaker enforced the thought that God's mercy will not exempt man from duty—that in grace as in nature there is a human as well as a divine part.

Mr. Shaw is marked by several peculiarities. He is a tall, raw-boned man, possesses great powers of endurance, and is deeply in earnest. He intersperses the sermon with many pointed anecdotes, and makes some powerful hits at pop-

> *ular sins — in short, a live preacher; and though one may differ from him and object to his eccentricities, he will nevertheless admit he is a power for good. Mr. Shaw will hold open-air services again in Lafayette Square next Sunday evening."*

After a few days' rest, which with him meant more than an ordinary man's work, he again visited Memphis, where he remained two weeks engaged in active labor, which resulted in nine additions to the church. Less than one week after this he was at Jackson, Mississippi, where he continued two weeks, holding sometimes three and even four services per day; some of them in the open air, Twenty-eight were added to the church, and many recruits obtained for the temperance army.

The Jackson *Times* thus noticed his meetings:

> *Services were held at the Christian Church on yesterday morning, and again at night. Both were well attended, especially at night. when the house was filled to overflowing, many persons having to stand outside at the doors and windows. The theme was the "Trial and Crucifixion of Christ," which was presented in a peculiarly unique manner. At the close of the services one young lady presented herself for membership, three persons having done so at the morning services, making a total to this date of nineteen persons who have united themselves with that church during this meeting. The minister in charge, Rev. Knowles Shaw, is certainly a man of no ordinary abilities, and we hope that his visit to Jackson will result in great good to the cause of religion here.*

And again:

> *Rev. Knowles Shaw, the Evangelist, is still here and his meetings are becoming daily more interesting. Tremendous crowds of all classes, conditions, and denominations are attracted to his services. The open-air meeting in front of the Capitol, on Sunday afternoon, at 6 o'clock, was the largest of the kind we have ever seen in Jackson. He preached a powerful sermon and was listened to with marked attention. In the evening, at 8 o'clock, he held forth*

> in the Christian Chapel to a house overflowing with attentive and eager listeners. Mr. Shaw is certainly a man of ability, of extraordinary musical powers, and his services are of such a character as to attract the attention of all classes. He will remain in this city for two or three days yet, and we would advise all who have not heard him yet to do so without delay.

From Jackson the unwearied laborer returned home, and did a good work for the church at Columbus, and, adding some to its number, thence, on the 29th of June, to West Point, Mississippi, where he labored for one week; and, after an interval of a few days, we find him at Saltillo, Mississippi, and, in a meeting of twelve days, had thirty-four additions. On the 27th of July he began a meeting at Henderson, Tennessee, which continued one week; thirteen added; and on the 4th of August, another at Lynnville, Tennessee, of ten days; seventeen added.

We next find him, after being one day at home, at Baldwyn, Mississippi, from August 17th to the 29th; added six there; and was at Lawrenceburg, Indiana, on the 1st of September; preached eighteen days, with but two additions. The next three days preached at three places: Mount Pleasant, Harrison, Ohio, and Rushville. Next preached four times in two days at Little Flat Rock, Indiana; and, after five days at home, started for Mount Sterling, Kentucky, which he reached September 5th, and preached nearly three weeks, with twenty-one additions. After a single day's rest he began a meeting at Covington, Kentucky; had fine hearing, and twelve additions. A trip to his old home in Kansas gave him a few days of needed rest. He reached his home in Mississippi on the 23rd of November, and between that and the 17th of December delivered some fourteen vigorous discourses at home. The 8th of December is the only day in the year which I find devoted to recreation. His last meeting for the year was at Henderson, Tennessee, which did not terminate until after the close of the year.

He preached four hundred and sixty-four times; in the intervals between his sermons talked almost incessantly, made the personal acquaintance of a vast number of people, visited the sick, worked in the temperance cause as if that were his whole employment, composed music, and sang a number of times every day, more indeed than if he had been a professional singer, and added to the churches at various points two hundred and twenty persons, nearly all of whom he baptized with his own hands. More than once at a single meeting he had more converts than during this entire year; in one instance two hundred and twenty-six in a meeting of three weeks' duration. But even this year shows work such as but few men have been willing to undertake, and which still fewer have been able to accomplish.

The next year, 1878, possesses a mournful interest. Before the half of it had passed this great toilers work was done. The first two days of the year were spent in a meeting at Henderson, Tennessee, and on the 3rd of January he started for Paris, Kentucky. The meeting there continued nearly four weeks; large crowds came out to hear him. The daily entries in his diary show a very humble and prayerful spirit. There were two baptisms of special interest: one a little girl ten years of age, the other a man eighty-one years of age. During the meeting a man was shot in a drinking saloon, which caused him to say: "I feel more and more determined to fight the demon intemperance, the chief foe of religion and morality." Sixty-five additions were the visible results of the meeting.

He reached home on the 2nd of February, and remained until March the 15th. During this time he inaugurated the "Murphy" temperance movement, amid great opposition and intense excitement. His lectures and songs were irresistible; large crowds gathered wherever he spoke; the whole city was agitated, and in about six weeks nearly two thousand persons signed the pledge. He then preached a week at Madison, Mississippi, and went thence to Jackson, in the same State; addressing great crowds during his stay. Here, he also started the temperance work, with gratifying results; as many as one hundred signing the pledge at a single meeting. On the 30th of March he visited Aberdeen, preached with success, and aroused the whole community on the temperance question, inducing many to sign.

On the 13th of April he came home; which proved to be his last visit to his loved and dear ones. I call it a visit, because his arduous and abundant labors kept him away from his family by far the greater portion of his time. How he spent those few last days may be a matter of interest. Like all the rest of his time, they were spent in earnest efforts to do good. The following extracts from his diary tell of his endeavors and success:

> *Sunday, April 14, 1878, 9 A.M. Sunday-school good. 10½ A.M., preached. Subject, 'Go Forward.' Stormy. 3 P.M., preached. Subject, 'State Privilege and Character.' (Romans 8:1.) 7½ P.M. Crowded house. Subject, 'Commission.' Two confessions; grand.*
>
> *Monday, 15th, 7½ P.M. Subject, 'True Road to Happiness.' One confession.*
>
> *Tuesday, 16th, 4 P.M. Subject, Romans 6:4. Baptized three persons. Same evening lectured on Temperance. Forty-seven signed the pledge.*
>
> *Wednesday, 17th, 4 P.M. Subject, Romans 5:1. Baptized one. 7½ P.M. Preached on 'The Power of God.' Good audience.*
>
> *Thursday, 18th, 7½ P.M. Preached on 'Sufficiency of Revelation.'*
>
> *Friday, 19th. Stormy. Preached on 'Zeal.' (2 Corinthians 2:3.)*
>
> *Saturday, 20th. Preached 7½ P.M., on 'Election.'*
>
> *Sunday 21st. Sunday-school 9½ A.M. Preached at 10½. Subject, 'Glad Tidings.' 3 P.M. Spoke on 'Evils of Drunkenness.' Eleven signed the pledge. At 7 P.M., preached on 'Freedom by the Truth.' Monday, 22nd, 7 P.M. Preached. Subject, 'Moses' hands held up.'*
>
> *Tuesday, 23rd. Temperance meeting.*
>
> *Wednesday, 24th. Preached. Subject, 'Christ our King.'*
>
> *Sunday, 28th. Sunday-school at 9 A.M. Preached at 10½ A.M. Subject, 'God revealed in Christ, and man reconciled to God.'"*

This was the last Lord's Day with his home church and family. His theme in the morning was one which called forth all his powers, the glory of God as seen in Christ; the fearful danger of man through sin, unless reconciled through Christ, seemed vividly present. He said: "It is only in obedience to the divine law that man can reap the benefits from the life of love, and death-sacrifice of Christ. Indeed, no man can justly claim to be reconciled to God who is not willing to cease from his sin and yield his will and life to God; for the evidence of reconciliation is—subjection to the law of God." He then set forth in language of the Scriptures, and closed with an exhortation to be reconciled to God *now,* on the terms set forth in his truth. And then, as if the "dark event," not distant, "cast its shadow before," he added: "I can not close this sermon till I thank you for your good wishes for my safety while away. How often will I think of you! If I never live to get back, I feel pretty sure I'll go straight home to Jesus, by whom, twenty-four years ago, I was reconciled to God." Then, making a last appeal to the unconverted portion of his audience, he said: "All our days are fast passing away; and oh, the thought of meeting God in the judgment, without reconciliation—an enemy! To be banished for ever! Hear the word of reconciliation now: 'O turn ye, O turn ye, for why will you die?' The Savior calls, Mercy pleads, the Spirit woos, and the Father smiles, while all glory beams, and angels are ready to rejoice. *Come, while you may."*

One who was present says of the discourse: "Nothing I ever heard could exceed the pathos and tenderness of that sermon; and so heart-aching is the memory of it, now that it is coupled with a mournful realization, almost makes me wish I had never heard it. The scene as now recalled was not unlike that when Paul parted from the church at Ephesus, when he told them that he would never return; and they sorrowed most of all for the words he spake, that they should see his face no more."

At 7½ P.M., the same evening, he preached on the "Fullness of Times." One confession, seventy years old; the tenth one received of that age.

Tuesday, 30th, 4 P.M. Subject, "Self-Examination." Immersed Mr. and Mrs. Cline. 8 P.M. Preached on "Great Salvation." Six confessions.

Wednesday, May 1st, 4 P.M. Baptismal service. Preached on "Harvest." (Galatians 6:7.) With this theme and the baptism of six converts, he closed his work at Columbus, and left the next day for Dallas, Texas, never to return.

Chapter Fifteen

*Brother Shaw's Last Meeting—His Last Day—
An Account of the Wreck.*

A peculiar interest is connected with Brother Shaw's last meeting, an account of which has been prepared by Elder Kirk Baxter, who was the pastor of the church at Dallas at that time, and not only took part in the meeting, but was with him in the disaster by which his useful life was ended. He thus briefly tells the story:

ELDER KNOWLES SHAW'S LAST MEETING.

The earthly labors of this gifted and successful evangelist terminated in a meeting of five weeks with the Commerce Street Christian Church, Dallas, Texas. Arrangements having been made with him a month before for a meeting, to commence on the 4th of May, 1878, he arrived promptly at the time, direct from his home, Columbus, Mississippi. Several brethren met him at the depot, and conducted him to the residence of Brother L.D. Myers, one of Brother Shaw's converts in Kansas, and a deacon of the church here. Quite a number had assembled at the house to greet him, although it was late at night. He soon was engaged in earnest conversation, and had a good word for all present. We spent an hour with him, and heard him sing some of his grand songs. The next morning (Lord's Day) a large audience greeted him in our new meeting-house. His first discourse was a grand effort on 'The Furtherance of the Gospel.' All went away delighted with the preacher and his sermon. At night the house would not accommodate the people who thronged to hear him. His service of song, thirty minutes before each sermon, prepared the hearts of the people to receive the truth he had to present. Thus the meeting went on from day to day, commencing promptly at 10 o'clock A.M., and 8 P.M., and I do not think that he varied a moment during the entire meeting. After he had preached several sermons he was asked what he thought as to the success of the meeting. His reply was: 'That depends very largely upon the work you have done; the preparation you made before I came. To make the meeting a success we must all work, and work together. It is not my meeting, but our meeting, and we must all do our part to make it what it ought to be, and what it will be if we do our duty.' His 'morning talks,' as he called them, were intensely practical and heart-searching, and caused many a lukewarm Christian to tremble as he held up their short-comings before them. In these 'talks' there were always two characteristics of this extraordinary man standing out prominently, namely, his devotion to the truth, and his courage in exposing sin wherever he found it. He made his audience feel that he was talking to them, and not to some imaginary crowd. He called evil, evil, and good, good; and his whole effort was to bring his hearers up to a higher and better life. During the interval between the morning and evening meetings he literally went every day from the pulpit to the street, to the work-shop, to the counting-room, to the by-ways and hedges, to all parts of the city, and would come to his work at night full of incidents and illustrations that he had gathered up in his rambles. He had a kind word for every one he met, and the result was that crowds came to hear him preach who never before had taken an interest in the gospel. I never saw a man who had such power over the people. Men who had not been in a church for ten or fifteen years came night after night. Members of other churches, who had been so prejudiced that they would not hear our people, came, and would say of the preaching, 'It is true; it is just what the Bible teaches.'

His work went on grandly in this way for five successive weeks, during which he received calls from various parts of the State to go and hold meetings; also some urgent calls from California. The interest increased to the last, and the immediate result was one hundred and twelve additions to the church. His last 'morning talk' was on the death of

Moses. He said he hoped that God would not permit him to outlive his usefulness; that he wanted to die in the strength of manhood, with the harness on; that if he could have his wish he would like to go from the pulpit to glory; but, if not, he wanted to die suddenly.

The last night of the meeting was peculiarly solemn and impressive. The house was crowded to overflowing, and many gathered outside to catch the last strain of song and hear his last words. His sermon was one of his grandest efforts. He then gave his farewell talk, which proved to be his last public utterance on earth. He said that we were soon to separate, never to meet on earth; that we knew not who would be taken first; it may be myself, it may be your beloved pastor; God alone knows. Some of us may be dead in less than twenty- four hours. His closing remarks were beautiful— his charge to the preacher, officers and members, to the young converts, to the world—indeed, to all present, for he forgot no one—was deeply impressive. Finally, he asked forgiveness, if in his zeal for the truth, he had wounded the feelings of any one, and, kneeling down, he offered one of the most beautiful and touching prayers that I ever heard. He then sang the following song:

> *When my final farewell to the world I have said,*
> *And gladly lie down to my rest:*
> *hen softly the watchers shall say, 'He is dead,'*
> *And fold my pale hands o'er my breast;*
> *And when, with my glorified vision at last*
> *The walls of 'that city' I see,*
> *Will any one then at the beautiful gate*
> *Be waiting and watching for me?*

> "*There are little ones glancing about in my path,*
> *In want of a friend and a guide:*
> *There are dear little eyes looking up into mine,*
> *Whose tears might be easily dried;*
> *But Jesus may beckon the children away*
> *In the midst of their grief and their glee—*
> *Will any one, then, at the beautiful gate,*

     Be waiting and watching for me?

  "There are old and forsaken who linger awhile
   In homes which their dearest have left;
  And a few gentle words or an action of love
   May cheer their sad spirits bereft.
  But the Reaper is near to the long-standing corn,
   The weary will soon be set free —
  Will any one then at the beautiful gate
   Be waiting and watching for me?

  "Oh, should I be brought there by the bountiful grace
   Of Him who delights to forgive:
  Though I bless not the weary about on my path,
   Pray only for self while I live,
  Methinks I should mourn o'er my sinful neglect,
   If sorrow in heaven could be;
  Should no one I love at the beautiful gate
   Be waiting and watching for me?"

  After this, the audience then nearly all weeping, were dismissed, yet they lingered to take him once more by the hand, and receive from him a warm "God bless you." The last farewell was said, and the noble worker's work was done.

  From the same hand we have an account of Brother Shaw's last day, and tragical death. He writes:

> *Cleburne, Texas, June 7, 1879.*
>
> *Dear Brother:— Just one year ago, today, Brother Shaw was killed. During his last meeting among the numerous calls to labor at other places, was one from the church at McKinney, which sent a delegation to urge him to visit there, if only for a few days. He replied, 'As that is one of Brother Baxter's points of labor, I will go.' His meeting at Dallas closed on the night of the 6th of June. That night he spent at Brother Dr. Johnston's. He telegraphed to the church at McKinney, that he and I would be there the next day. Early the next morning there was a tremendous rain-fall, lasting two or three hours. The brethren tried to prevail on him not to go to McKinney that morning, urging*

that the weather was so unfavorable that he could not have a meeting if he went, and insisted that he should remain in Dallas that day and rest. He replied, 'No; we have telegraphed the brethren we would be there, and we must go;' that there was no time for rest now; rest would come by and by. I met him at the depot about seven o'clock that morning, as lively and cheerful as I ever had seen him. He had bought his ticket and was ready to start. We took a seat in the car, and, in a few moments, were off. We conversed a few moments in regard to the work at McKinney. He then took up the morning paper and looked through it. While thus engaged, I left him, and went forward to the front of the car, and was about to pass out to the coach ahead, when some one called me by name. I turned, and saw a Methodist minister, Mr. Malloy, whom I had known years before in Arkansas. I sat down by him, and spent some time in conversation. He asked me about our meeting in Dallas, and Brother Shaw. I told him that Mr. Shaw was on the train, and just at that moment caught his eye, and beckoned to him, and he came to where we were seated. I introduced him to Rev. Mr. Malloy, and gave him my seat, and took the next one. Mr. Malloy asked him to tell him the secret of his success in protracted meetings, which Brother Shaw proceeded to do in a very earnest manner, saying he depended much on the power of a song-preached Christ; always kept Jesus before the people; made them feel that they were sinners, and needed just such a Savior as he preached; that he never became discouraged; had confidence in the gospel truth as the power of God; that he loved his work, and became wholly absorbed in it; and added: 'Oh, it is a grand thing to rally people to the Cross of Christ.' At that moment, I turned to see if we were in sight of McKinney, and I felt the car was off the track, bouncing over the ties. I did not feel in any danger; did not know that we were on an embankment, and expected that we would check up in a moment or two. I saw Brother Shaw rise from his seat, and realized at once that the car was going over. Not a word was spoken. I saw Brother Shaw alive no more. All became as dark as night. When I came to myself, the coach was at the bottom of the embankment, and I was its only occupant.

I looked round, but all were gone. When I got out, I saw the passengers on the railroad track above me, and made my way up to them. The first one I met was Mr. Malloy, with whom Brother Shaw was seated at the time of the accident. I said to him, 'Have you seen Brother Shaw.' 'No,' said he, 'I fear he is under the wreck; but he saved my life by pushing me from the position in which he himself fell.' I waited to hear no more, but ran down to the wreck, looked in, and saw a man's hand pointing upward out of the water. It was Brother Shaw's hand. I called for help, and in about fifteen minutes he was taken lifeless from the water. Portions of the wreck had to be cut away with an ax before the body could be reached and removed. I had the body placed in the baggage-car, which had not been thrown from the track, and sent to McKinney, where it was taken charge of by the brethren and placed in the church. I sent a telegram to Dallas, telling the sad news. In a short time, a deep gloom pervaded the whole city, as from house to house passed the sad words, 'Brother Shaw is dead.' Quite a number were injured by the accident; some very severely. My own injuries were of a serious nature, much more so than I at first supposed. Such was Brother Shaw's last day on earth.

Kirk Baxter.

The Dallas papers, of June the 8th, give the following account of the wreck:

A disastrous accident to the north-bound passenger train, on the Houston and Texas Central Railroad, occurred about two miles south of McKinney, at a quarter past nine o'clock yesterday morning, which was attended with death and destruction.

The train consisted of engine, baggage and mail car, two passenger coaches, and a sleeper, and was running at usual speed. Arriving at the point designated, which was on an embankment about forty feet high, and near Wilson's Creek, a broken rail precipitated the rear coach and the sleeper down the embankment, and completely wrecked that part of the train. All the other parts ran over the break in the road, and were not materially damaged. The first news received of the accident was a telegram to Captain C.M. Wheat from Elder Kirk Baxter, pastor of the Christian Church here, breaking the startling intelligence, that Elder Knowles Shaw, who was in company with him aboard the train, was killed outright, and requesting him to come up at once.

A number of telegrams were sent and received during the morning, yet the answers received were rather vague and contradictory. Throughout the day there was great anxiety felt in this city, as a majority of the passengers had friends here who were desirous of knowing the fate of the passengers after the first news of the accident had been confirmed.

The very latest and fullest account, both by telegraph and from reporters detailed to go to the scene of the accident, is to the effect that there were in all twenty-seven persons more or less wounded, and one killed. Of the wounded, the following names are those who were at McKinney, at the American House, late yesterday evening; the others having gone north on the train which went on to its destination in an hour or so after the accident. Those whose names do not appear in the list of wounded, received slight bruises only.

WOUNDED.

Rev. George W. Henry, of Denison, severely about the head.

Mrs. Aggie, wife of G.W. Henry, severely about the head.

Miss Katie Henry, slightly.

G.W. Henry, Jr., slightly.

Miss Carry Spooner, of Denison, about the head, slightly.

Miss Augusta Stidman, deaf mute, from asylum at Austin, slightly.

Rev. J.T. Miller, of Ennis, severely.

Albert Billings, sleeping-car porter, slightly.

Elder Kirk Baxter, of Dallas, about the head and chest, dangerously.

George Mountcastle, postmaster at Allen, dangerously.

S.C. Anderson, employe of R.V. Tompkins, Dallas, slightly.

Conductor Lasher, rib broken and some slight bruises.

Rev. W.L. Malloy, of Sherman, slightly.

Some one, name unknown, from Mineola, slightly.

KILLED.

No one was killed but Elder Knowles Shaw, of Mississippi. Mr. Shaw arrived here on the 4th day of May last, under an engagement of the Commerce Street Christian Church to conduct a revival, which was continued thirty-three days and nights, during which time he delivered sixty-six discourses. The result of his efforts was one hundred and eleven additional members to the church.

From a prominent member of the Christian Church of this city, it is learned that Mr. Shaw was born in the State of Ohio, in 1834, and, at an early age, moved to Indiana. Shortly after, his father died and left him at the head of the family. At the age of seventeen years he joined the Christian Church, shortly after which he began preaching; and, if he had lived until the 1st day of next January, he would have been preaching twenty- one years. The past fifteen years of his life have been spent as an evangelist, and in supporting and helping various churches. At the age of twenty-three years, he married a Miss Finley, of Virginia, and continued to reside in Indiana up to a short time ago, when he moved to Columbus, Mississippi. He leaves a wife and two children—a young lady about nineteen years old, and a youth about sixteen years old. He was very successful as a revivalist; and had attained some notoriety in the Northern and Western States for his success in this line, and for his compilation of Sunday-school songs.

Mr. Shaw, at the time of the accident, was sitting in the passenger coach talking with Rev. Mr. Malloy, to whom he was introduced a short time before by Elder Baxter. Mr. Malloy says Mr. Shaw saved his (Malloy's) life by grabbing him and pushing him away from the position in which he fell himself. Mr. Shaw's right arm was broken in two or three places; there is a severe cut on top of his head, one on the forehead, slightly on the nose, and his lower limbs were badly mangled and his neck broken.

Elder Baxter, when he came to the car, looked for Mr. Shaw, and found him entangled in the wreck, and partly covered with water. It took fifteen minutes to extricate his body by cutting around it with an ax. His body was taken care of by friends at McKinney, where it was washed and dressed, and laid out in a handsome coffin. It was brought to this city last evening, where it was taken to Willett & Smith's and embalmed. It will be kept here awaiting orders from his family as to its disposition.

He kept a register of the number of those converted under his ministrations, which, in round numbers, is over eleven thousand.

Night before last, he preached his farewell sermon to the congregation of the Commerce Street Christian Church, of this city; and, when killed, was on his way to McKinney to hold a protracted meeting. The news of his death was a severe blow to his many friends in this city, as he was held in high esteem by all who knew him.

The train, at the time of the accident, was on a curve, and about three hundred yards south of the bridge over the creek. The passenger coach turned over twice, and is now bottom upwards in a ditch, and a complete wreck. The sleeper turned over twice, and is lying on one side. Most of the passengers were in the coach.

A party of thirty went to care for the wounded. Drs. Hughes, Leak, Graham, Johnson, and Allen, all of this city, did effective service in alleviating the suffering of the wounded."

Thus perished, in the prime of life and in the midst of his usefulness, our beloved brother; and we feel quite safe in saying that no death among our brotherhood ever called forth profounder grief. He was at the time of his death within four months of being forty-four years of age, with a vigorous constitution, the full and free use of all his powers, a rich experience, and, if possible, with a greater desire than ever for the salvation of his fellow-men.

The funeral rites were of a peculiarly solemn character. Memorial services were held in several States. Various bodies, benevolent and religious, united in expressing their admiration of his work and worth, and sorrow for his loss. His last words: "Oh, it is a grand thing to rally the people to the Cross of Christ," became the motto of many a tender speech, many a touching poem, many a stirring song.

A volume might be filled with the varied tributes to his memory, but want of space forbids more than an abridged account of the funeral services, and a flower gathered here and there from the wreaths of eloquence and song which love and friendship strewed upon his grave.

Chapter Sixteen

Funeral Services at Dallas—Closing Services, and Burial at Rushville, Indiana.

From McKinney, as already stated, the remains of the departed one were taken to Dallas, and placed in the church, where he had but a short time before so earnestly and successfully labored. On the next day (Lord's Day), June the 9th, the funeral services took place, which were noticed as follows in the city papers:

"THE LAST RITES.
"FUNERAL SERVICES OF MR. SHAW, SUNDAY MORNING. AN IMMENSE CONCOURSE PAY TRIBUTE TO HIS MEMORY.

As early as nine o'clock Sunday morning people began to gather within the building where lay all that was earthly of the dead evangelist. The casket was profusely decorated with odorous flowers, while scattered upon the floor beneath it were immense bunches of incense breathing roses, geraniums, honeysuckles, and clippings from the rarest gardens in the city. On the stand, in the rear, a dozen or more vessels, filled with beautiful plants and evergreens, were tastefully arranged. Crosses, anchors, and other elegantly worked floral designs were strewn upon the lid of the coffin \ but none were there more elegant than the crown of roses brought by Mrs. Dr. A.A. Johnston. This was placed near the head, and an open Bible rested against it. In a line of green letters above the altar, was, 'Fell at his post,' underneath which were three large pictures of the deceased; and below the largest—the center picture—was a placard containing his last words: 'It is a grand thing to rally people to the Cross of Christ.'

As the minutes sped on, the crowd continued to gather in great numbers, until the large audience-room was packed

135

to its utmost. Chairs were placed in the aisles, and still the immense congregation could not be accommodated. A little before eleven o'clock, Mr. Smith, the organist, took his position at the instrument, and began to send out upon the air, in low and solemn cadence, that sweetest of all sounds in music, 'Home, Sweet Home.' As the mournful strains of the voluntary rose, gathered, and fell, the vast audience seemed to realize indeed the full force of the occasion, and strong men wept. Rarely has a more affecting scene been witnessed than that which marked the exercises at this time.

At eleven o'clock, Elder J.T. Bly, of Knoxville, Iowa, ascended the platform, and began the opening service by reading the fifteenth chapter of First Corinthians. The opening song, to music of Mr. Shaw's own composition, was: 'If thou, Lord, callest me;' and, as the organ pealed forth the solemn notes, full many an eye was wet with weeping, and tears of sympathy rolled down the cheeks of strangers as well as those who knew and loved him well.

Prayer was then offered by Dr. Armstrong, of the Tabernacle. His appeal in behalf of the absent wife and bereaved children was a tearful offering of love and affection. Eloquently simple, and tenderly pathetic, his words fell with soft and soothing force upon all who heard them. Another of Mr. Shaw's songs—'Beyond the Dark Sea'—was then rendered, and Mr. Bly delivered the funeral discourse.

This effort, delivered under trying circumstances, was a masterly one; and when we give a skeleton of it this morning, we feel that, in doing so, we do neither the speaker nor the occasion justice. It should have been heard to be appreciated.

The text was chosen from Acts 26:8: 'Why should it seem a thing incredible with you that God should raise the dead?' His subject was 'The Credibility of the Resurrection.' He announced, that with the resurrection the claims of Jesus and the Bible stand or fall. It is at the door of the sepulcher that hope lingers with the inquiry: 'Is he here?' The angel and the empty tomb echo back, 'Not here; He is risen.' God, in the nature of things, made no provision for sin. Therefore, the nature of things can furnish no remedy for sin and its consequences. Science can only discover the difficulty. The herald note of the gospel—the 'so loved' is the overture—the arbitrary divine intervention that brings to man the remedy. The revelation of Jesus the Christ is the solution of the great problem of life and happiness. In Him we have the complete harmonization of God and man; therefore the unalterable conditions of life endless, and happiness unalloyed. While Nature and Science walk hand in hand, the revelation of the crucified and risen Savior calls for faith.

The resurrection is credible—

1st. God is able to raise the dead.

2nd. The happy result of this revelation upon the lips and character of the laborer, bears testimony, calling out the nobler faculties of his being—faith, hope, and love— assimilating him to the divine character.

3rd. The responsiveness of the resurrection bears testimony—

a. It responds to man's desire for life. Job's question, 'If a man die, shall he live again?' is a living question. The vacated tomb says, **'he shall live again.'**

b. It represents the Christian's hope of immortality. As the divine nature has permeated his spiritual nature, and molded him into the likeness of the character of the Savior; so in the resurrection shall he be permeated entire—made incorruptible. It responds to the Christian's aspirations for happiness. Having an approved character, an incorruptible body, he is fitted for happiness to the utmost of his possibilities.

The denial of the resurrection—

1st. Ignores the Bible as a revelation from God.

2nd. Converts the mission of Christ into the arch deception of the world. The devil appeals to our carnal nature and promises reward here. Jesus appeals to our spiritual nature and promises eternal reward. If he did not rise again, he has out-generaled the devil as a deceiver.

3rd. Involves the testimony of history. The name Jesus is the great historic name of literature—in Christian literature the greatest. Of Christian civilization—the best ever known in the world's history.

CONCLUSION.

The denial of the resurrection closes the gates of immortality, and the grave of the eternal Sleeper, and reduces man's existence to a monstrosity. Has God mocked man by imbuing in his nature the conditions to infinite possibilities and aspirations, equal in their measure without any conditions whatever of their realization? 'Now, is Christ risen from the dead?' This is our hope.

Brother Shaw's work of faith and labor of love closed with the Dallas meeting. We can pass no higher eulogy upon him than to say he needs none. He will ever stand before us in the bold outlines of an earnest devoted life. And while his cold inanimate form lies before us in the stillness of death, we are reminded that the echoes of his warning voice will not die away until they find rest on the farther shores of time. His work will go on. Such a life of faith is reproductive. Among the thousands who have responded to his earnest appeals, many will catch the gospel strain and send it along down the ages. The fact of his untimely death will but intensify that sense of responsibility that underlies every successful Christian life. How inexplicable that one of such rare combination should be called from labor to rest at noontide! May our kind Father, whose providential ways are beyond our view, overrule this sad dispensation to the future and greater good of those left behind.

After the delivery of the funeral discourse, Mr. Armstrong succeeded Mr. Bly; and, as the tender utterances fell from his lips, the congregation was again moved to tears.

Mr. Wheat, after making a short address, proposed that the congregation should kneel in a prayer of thankfulness that their pastor, Elder Kirk Baxter, who was with Mr. Shaw the day of the fearful disaster, was spared to them. In this prayer Mr. Armstrong led.

Mr. Baxter, who was present, but who had to be assisted into the church—the bruises on whose head and left eye were plainly discernible to those in the remotest seats in the church—was requested to tell the congregation how the terrible accident happened. This he did in tones that told he was suffering mental anguish as well as enduring physical pain; but as the account of the wreck has hitherto been published in these columns, we will not reproduce it.

Over the cold body of Mr. Shaw an appeal was made to sinners to turn to God, and four came forward and united themselves with the church. The hymn, 'Fallen on Zion's Battle Field—a Soldier of Renown,' was sung in conclusion of the services. After the audience was dismissed, a large number of persons pressed forward to view the body.

The remains continued to lie in state in the church until yesterday morning; when, attended by weeping friends, they were taken to the depot, and sent, on the 7:20 train, under care of Mr. L.D. Myers, to Rushville, Indiana, for burial. So has gone out of life a noble man of God—a gallant warrior from the host of Israel."

During Brother Shaw's meeting at Dallas, in one of his sermons, he said: "If I should die while I am here, I want you to send my body to Rushville, Indiana, for burial." His request was complied with, as above stated; and Brother L.D. Myers, who attended to this kind yet sad office, tells, in the following letter to the *Christian Standard*, how his mournful mission was discharged:

Dear Brother Errett:—I returned home from my sorrowful trip to Rushville, Indiana, with the remains of Brother Shaw, last Thursday. I arrived in Rushville on Wednesday, 12th inst., about nine A.M., and found a large assembly of sorrowing friends and relatives of our good brother who met me at the depot. His poor old mother was there, heart-broken, as is perfectly natural, to have so dutiful and worthy a son brought home under such circumstances. But she said, only a few short years and she would join him in the bright beyond.

His wife, son, and daughter did not arrive for a few hours, having missed connection at Cincinnati. They, too, came with sorrowful hearts; but Sister Shaw was more resigned than I expected to find her. She is a strong-minded, sensible woman, and seemed to be equal to the emergency. For years she has been expecting something of the kind to happen; as he lived, when not in the church house, on the rail. She had almost given him up; or, in other words, he belonged to the church and people. He was always in a meeting. When away from home, engaged in meetings (which was nearly all the time), he delivered two sermons per day, three on Lord's days, besides two singing rehearsals per day of one-half to one hour each. Then, when he returned home, he entered the pulpit and continued in one grand protracted meeting until called to another point. Remarkable man, never satisfied only when singing or preaching the everlasting gospel of Christ.

Last winter, while I was corresponding with him with reference to the meeting just ended, I received a postal card from him, urging the members here to hold a prayer service for a week or ten days prior to the meeting, so that when he came he might begin at once, and not have to work a week to commence. Said he, I have no fears of converts if members are aroused to do their duty, winding up the postal-card thus:

> *'Yours with great sticktoitiveness and neverletgoitiveness,'*
>
> *'K. Shaw.'*

From about eight years' acquaintance with him, I thought that combination of words gave a free expression of the man and his life. But, will return to the narrative of my trip.

Thursday, 13th instant, was set for funeral service. The day at hand, it was soon discovered that no building would hold the people; so the remains were taken to Court-house Square. The crowd that gathered there I did not hear estimated, but it was the largest I ever witnessed on a similar occasion. The services were conducted by Brother J.M. Conner. Brother L.H. Jameson, of Indianapolis—that good old veteran in the cause of Christ—delivered the memorial discourse, in which he stated that he was preaching four years before Brother Shaw was born; had known him from boyhood; had been for years side by side with him in the grand work. One feature of his life he wished to emphasize: 'That in all his (Brother Shaw's) intercourse with men and women, since he entered the ministry, not one charge was ever brought against his character.' The speaker continued, 'What a pattern for his co-laborers left behind to follow!' Some twenty or more preachers were present, among whom I noticed Brothers J.M. Conner, L.H. Jameson, James Conner, Jr., J.W. Conner, H.R. Pritchard, Jacob Daubenspeck, E.L. Frazee, D.L. Thomas (son of Brother George Thomas, who immersed Brother Shaw), Walter S. Campbell, Jacob Blount, Dr. Jas. Orr, J.W. Ferrell, L.D. McGowen, N. Marlott, Methodist Episcopal, Mr. Hutchinson, United Presbyterian. Nearly all had something to say, praising the life and good work of the man whose lifeless form lay silent before them.

The H. & T.C. Railroad granted passes to Sedalia, Missouri, and return. There I was met by Brother Ragland, the pastor at Sedalia, and the elders, who rendered assistance to St. Louis. There I was met by Brothers Garrison, Burns, and Renshaw, who rendered valuable assistance to Indianapolis. Thanks to them, also to the brethren at Rushville and Big Flat Rock, in Rush County, for contributions to help defray expense of the journey. Funeral over, I remained with Brother Shaw's family until Monday morning. Came to Indianapolis; spent afternoon and night with Brother Jameson. Next day came to St. Louis; spent a few happy hours with Brother Garrison and family. At 9:15 started for home; arrived on Thursday; found Brother Baxter still suffering in mind and body, but he thinks he will recover. Thursday night went to prayer-meeting at Commerce Street Church, where Brother Shaw had so recently held such a good meeting. It was the largest and most interesting prayer-meeting I ever attended—some of the young converts praying and exhorting in public. Four additions to the church since the meeting. Thus the evangelistic work of our lamented brother goes on. Though dead, his life is before us; and his works, like bread cast upon waters, will be seen many, many days hence. Am trespassing upon your columns, but the request of many brethren and friends, urging me to report through the Standard, is the only apology I have for troubling your columns.

Your brother in Christ,

Dallas, Texas, June 25.

L.D. Myers.

The following account of the final funeral services is taken from the Rushville *Republican:*

Memorial Service at the Courthouse Park, Tuesday, June 13th, 1878.

At half-past ten o'clock there assembled about two thousand citizens of Rush County, in the Courthouse Park, to engage in memorial services to the memory of Elder Knowles Shaw; and the deep solemnity which pervaded the vast assembly, and the sympathy expressed, indicated how highly the deceased was loved and esteemed. No accident has ever happened to a citizen of Rush County that has so filled the hearts of the people with sorrow and sadness as this one. The friends erected a platform and temporary seats for about fifteen hundred persons. Immediately in front of the platform was a catafalque, which was handsomely decorated with flowers and evergreens. At the head was a life-size portrait of the deceased, and near it a card framed in evergreen, upon which was printed the last words of Knowles Shaw: 'It is a grand thing to rally people to the

Cross of Christ.' The casket was very handsomely decorated with flowers and evergreens, among which we noticed a cross of white roses, an anchor of evergreens and flowers, a beautiful wreath of magnolia blossoms from the Sunny South, furnished by Miss Lenora Norris, besides numerous other floral decorations from other loving friends. The exercises began with a duet, 'Only a Little While,' composed by the deceased, and sung by the Misses Norris. The manner in which it was rendered, and the sentiment of the song, left not a dry eye in the vast audience. Following this was the reading of various appropriate passages of Scripture by Elder D.L. Thomas; then a hymn by a very large choir, improvised for the occasion, and consisting of persons from the various churches. Dr. Orr, of Andersonville, followed, with an eloquent prayer. Elder J.W. Conner, of Crawfordsville, recently of Rushville, acted as officiating minister. Short eulogies were then pronounced upon the life and character of the deceased by Elders J.W. Conner, of Crawfordsville; L.H. Jameson, of Indianapolis; Jacob Daubenspeck, of Rush County; Walter S. Campbell, of Fairview; Rev. A.N. Marlatt, pastor of the Methodist Episcopal Church, Rushville, and L.D. Myers, Esq., of Dallas, Texas. The exercises at the Park closed with a song from 'Pure Gold' by the choir, entitled 'One by One we Gather,' when the funeral cortege proceeded to East Hill Cemetery, where the remains were buried. Eight ministers acted as pall-bearers.

So ended the last rites in memory of one who was dearly loved by all who knew him, and who, while in life, labored for the elevation of his race with untiring energy and zeal, and was stricken down in the midst of his usefulness and labor. Surely of such an one we can say, 'Death is the crown of life.'

Chapter Seventeen

Difference Between Our Judgments Concerning the Living and the Dead—Memorial Service at Columbus, Mississippi.

In the course of our narrative we have introduced the various opinions entertained of Brother Shaw while living—most of them just, no doubt, but some perhaps giving undue prominence to peculiarities which the writers would have regarded as unpardonable in themselves, but which formed an inseparable part of Brother Shaw's character, and may have in some degree contributed to his success. Many good preachers are unable to tell an anecdote in a manner acceptable to their hearers, while others can employ them in a way to give great point and force to their arguments; and very few are able to interject a moving song into their addresses. Both these Brother Shaw could do with admirable effect. In fact, the song and apt illustration were often the strong points of the sermon, making it far more effective than it could possibly have been had these been wanting. It was these that tipped the arrows of truth, as with flame, and feathered them so that they flew swiftly and surely until they hung quivering in the stricken heart. While living his methods occupied more attention than his work; since he has gone his work claims more of our attention than his methods; and in view of that work, finished, alas! too soon, much criticism, which in life seemed just, is disarmed; and there are few who would not be willing to subject themselves to criticism, far severer than he ever encountered, could they but leave a tithe of such blessed results behind. As winter's snow covers dead leaves, barren meadows, trunks of fallen trees, rough ravines, and unsightly ruts, in its stainless winding-sheet, so death hides all but the great outline of life, and leaves but the memory of that which is truest and best in the lives of those we shall see on earth no more.

Memorial services in honor of the dead evangelist were held at various places, where in life he had labored; but one service, held at Columbus, Mississippi, his home for some time preceding his death, will be found to be of peculiar interest. This meeting was held in the Christian Church, on the 14th of June, about one week after his tragical end, and was participated in by the ministers of the different churches, and other prominent personages. The Rev. Dr. Franklin was chairman of the meeting. The proceedings were in the following order:

MEMORIAL ADDRESSES.

Dr. Curtis said:

> *Responsive to the invitation of my church, I offer its humble tribute to the solemn services of this occasion. We come to strew flowers upon the tomb of our friend and brother; and to enter the Parthenon of the heart's best affections for oblations worthy of his memory. But the garlands which we bring, all blooming and fragrant with evergreen enamelings, are but silent symbols of heartswelling emotion that disdains the literature of speech. Such expressions, when language was impoverished and bankrupted for utterance, have distinguished civilized man in all ages, and under all forms of society. The Cecrops, the Mausoleum, the Taj Mahal, and Caecilia Mettela, were but so many silent tombs men erected to perpetuate the memory of the noble and venerated dead.*
>
> *And the pathway of Time is strewed with the debris of shattered and exfoliating monuments to dead styles of thought, dead forms of taste, of art, and literature, as well as dead heroes and distinguished dead men. There they stand and lie, magnificent in their ruins, in Torso beauty, but with the silent eloquence of the Elgin collection-types of eternal beauty.*
>
> *So our monumental meeting tonight, to do honor to the memory of Elder Knowles Shaw, is more to manifest what we feel, than to essay the formulation of that feeling in words. We would rather invoke the expressiveness and dignity of silence to declare his merits and avouch our grief.*
>
> *Elder Shaw, the inaugurator of the 'Murphy Movement' in our midst, and so beneficent in its results, is no more. His life-work is concluded, and the fruitage of nearly two years'*

of laborious efforts to meliorate the condition of man, and to promote the honor of God, is with us, as a rich and glorious legacy; and, though dead, and his ministries of love—in preaching, exhorting, singing, and praying with us—is lost to us forever, and the example of his pure and upright life is taken from us; yet in affection and in memory he is with us, and, as Abel from the slumbrous past speaks to the Christian heart, so Knowles Shaw speaks to us.

He was ever prompt in duty, earnest in action, zealous in the advocacy of truth, and pure in motive. He was rather a peculiar man, of undoubted genius, of wonderful memory, of boundless energy, and a faculty of hopefulness that threw an inspirational glamour over all the landscape of life, lighting it up with electric and poetic beauty. The very clouds of adversity all had bright silver linings to him. The normal condition of his being was that of happiness; and the boon he so much enjoyed himself, and which was as if his 'spirit was lapped in Elysium,' he desired all others to share; and, hence, becoming the center of a magic circle of social happiness, he diffused a paradise of pleasure wherever he was. The spell was enchantment; the fruitage, fruition.

His powers were all bent in the direction of virtue and unselfishness. He lived not for himself, but preeminently for others. He worked and talked and moved as one conscious of the obligation of existence, and apprehensive that life was too short to accomplish all of duty, and that what was to be done must be done quickly. His life was really an idyl—a poem of unselfish goodness and earnest usefulness. May we imitate his many virtues, emulate his noble zeal, and have embalmed in our hearts the forms of beauty and goodness that chastened and distinguished his valuable life. And, as no force is ever destroyed, as no thought ever dies, let us not despond or grow weary in the good work he begun. It will go on. It is the fiat of destiny. Let us assist in its progress and development.

And now, let us comfort our hearts in this very sad be-

reavement. The good are not only blessed in the transition of death, which is a mere change in the mode of being, but 'they rest from their labors, and their works do follow them.' As the sweetness of the perished rose lingers in the atmosphere around the parent stem, so do the labors and virtues of the dead exhale from the very tomb the freshness and fragrance of unsullied lives. The treasures of thought and learning conserved from the ravages of time in parchments, manuscripts, and books, in painting, sculpture, and architecture, are but a legacy bequeathed to us from preceding ages and generations of men for our use and happiness; and to be faithfully transmitted, unimpaired and improved, to succeeding generations. So of individual worth and merit. Everything in this world is fragmentary. One generation, and one individual, accomplish only so much, and another takes up the unfinished work and carries it on; and thus the cause of civilization and progress, as the cause of virtue, are carried forward, and the noblest ends of destiny achieved.

Knowles Shaw lives again in his teaching, in his example, and in the magnetic force left behind him. Death is but an episode in life; and, in the graceful style of one of the South's brightest sons, 'the limits even of time are overstepped, and the threads broken by death are woven in a new fabric beyond the stars. Not until the vast tapestry is unrolled before us in the pavilion of eternity itself, and the constituent figures are seen to be inwrought with an exquisite unity of design, shall we be able to frame a judgment of the wisdom of the whole.' But enough is known and appreciable to show the wonderful beauty of design, and to fix confidence in the benevolence and wisdom underlying those parts more occult and less understood. Thus we recognize all things to be for the best; and, to the devout heart, are felt to be a thing of beauty and a joy forever.

What is our loss is his gain; and how pleasant it is to feel that Knowles Shaw lives again, not only in the affections of those who loved him so well, but in the benignant smiles of that Savior whom he served so faithfully.

> *There's no such thing as death,*
> *To those who live aright;*
> *'Tis but the racer casting off*
> *What most impedes his flight.*
>
> *'Tis but one little act*
> *Life's drama must contain—*
> *One struggle greater than the rest,*
> *And then an end of pain.*
>
> *There's no such thing as death;*
> *That which is thus miscalled*
> *Is life escaping from the chains*
> *That have so long enthralled.*
>
> *'Tis but the bud displaced*
> *As comes the perfect flower;*
> *'Tis faith exchanged to sight,*
> *And weariness to power."*

Judge T.C. Lyon said:

> *In the collection of the antiquary there is to be found a medal struck by the city of Worms, in 1617. It represents a lighted candle shining upon the open Word, while a serpent endeavors to extinguish it; a hand from the skies points, indicating that divine strength feeds the flame; an inscription underneath signifies, 'O Lord, let it shine on forever.' The Truth, the Light, the Spirit of Evil, the Divine Protection, the Prayer of the Faithful! How fit an illustration this of the grand conflict between the Powers of Darkness and of Light, which now is, and has been, and will be until the millennial host triumphant shall crown earth's rightful King.*
>
> *But, alas, for mortal weakness! As the warrior sees, in the hard contest, the crest of some champion, triple-armed, unexpectedly sink, faith trembles, and, beholding, the expostulatory cry ascends, 'Could it not shine on, O Lord; can the dust praise thee; can it declare thy truth?'*
>
> *Is it to be denied but that with such feelings not a few in this presence and community regard the sudden extinguishment*

of the light of life and usefulness in him whose work among us, as humanitarian and Christian—as lover of his race and of his God—we are now here met to commemorate? But, the reflection comes, the temple of highest human hopes can not be marred by human loss; complete today as yesterday, no pillar can fall, nor stone of the corner crumble. God's work, as it regards man, in its every aspect, is his own; and his hand wars not against itself. By him, of him, and through him, are not only are all things permitted, but all things are. Stupendous thought! From eternity to eternity sweeps instant upon instant the eternal mind. It guides alike the rolling sun and the falling leaf; the shooting star and the floating azure speck. One of the greatest of mere men, captive upon the sea-girt rock, as he turned his eyes from the mighty past of his fallen fortunes, upward, exclaimed, 'Our days are reckoned?' So thought Napoleon in the days of rationalistic philosophy; and a greater hath spoken of the 'measure of his days,' and declared, 'my times are in thy hand.' No; the creative will did not commit his supreme work, with all its destinies, to blind, unmeaning chance, to be drifted black and blackening hell-ward. With a calm philosophy, therefore, let us believe the hand of Omniscience, and nothing short of it, marked the day of our friend's birth, and the day of his death, and the manner of that death as well. The logical idea of a perfect God demands the acknowledgment. To creature challenge, he replies: 'Be still, and know that I am God.'

The divine purpose in this death maybe to us inscrutable—the strong man falling in the midst of his strength—but could his voice now reach us from his seat of higher knowledge, doubtless it could and would unfold tremendous reason why. To you of his own flock, it might reveal a forbidden leaning upon an arm of flesh. He needeth not the strong; not since that time He sent the Galilean fishermen forth to make conquest of the world. Perhaps a glorying that was 'not all in the Lord;' perhaps in the hour of conscious weakness to strengthen faith; and, perhaps, by such and so terrible a death, to make the deeper impress of his teaching and example. These things, it might be, you would learn; but, of a surety, desponding hearts, Christ's own words to his sorrowing disciples would be his to you: 'It is expedient that I go away.'

To others, who knew him better, I leave a general analysis of the character of the departed; attempting only, in haste, to draw lessons that may be profitable to some from this sorrowful occasion. Nevertheless, I can not forbear to exalt, specially, two characteristics, plain to the passer-by, in the character of this, it must be confessed, extraordinary man: His devotion and his courage—the sword and buckler of the truth.

Knowles Shaw was, to some, a singular man, and singular in his ways. His idea of saving the souls and minds and bodies of his fellow-men, and augmenting the grand sum of temporal and eternal good during life's short span, differed from that of such, as duly once a week, with awful voice proclaim to immortals, heedlessly treading the crumbling verge of abysmal woes, without end, the gospel of the Son of God, as the sure, quick, and only escape, then, with as due awaiting, passed with polished hand and tongue of proper courtesy, and that alone, until the appointed time returns; aye, his practice differed. Consecrated, internally subjected, as it were, ardent, active, and continuing, the zeal of the Lord's house bore him from the pulpit to the street, to the place of business, to the work-shop, and, if needs be, to the gutter—hailing, persuading, urging, with affectionate solicitude, to reformation and a better life. 'Now,' blazoned in living light upon his breast, was the talismanic word of his action. Moreover, ye bear him witness, the woe is not of his calling, either express or by cowardly implication, light darkness, or darkness light. His bugle blast, and it was a blast, gave forth no uncertain sound on any question affecting man's highest welfare. He called evil, evil; and good, good. With a flash of the spirit of the Tishbite of old, he scouted Baal and his worshipers; and, with a boldness akin to that of the great worthies—from Peter and the Apostles to Luther, Calvin, John Knox, Bunyan, Wesley, and Whitfield—he hesitated not to declare, as he believed it, the whole counsel of God. Not hard is it to conceive, that had he lived in the days of the early church, prisons would have known him oft, and stonings, and scourgings, and the wild beasts of Ephesus, until through fire he had ascended to a martyr's crown.

The priceless value of the soul he seemed to feel as well as preach. To the eye following in that ceaseless round of his good work here, there, everywhere, at home, abroad, by day, by night, every day, every night, instant in season and out of season —his abounding labors expressed a conviction along with him, whose majestic thought proclaimed, that, were the sun to be clothed in sackcloth, and the moon to veil her face, all Nature could not utter a groan too deep to mark the calamity of a lost soul.

The record of the good done by the lamented, here in his charge, is written on the hearts of how many before me; the measure of his philanthropic labors in temperance reform, what numbers in this community can gratefully attest. There is need of no tongue of mine to tell. Before the man and his worlds were laid down the prejudices of years.

And, now, when we consider all, need we be surprised that eleven thousand converts marked the seventeen years of the ministry as evangelist of the Rev. Knowles Shaw! Eleven thousand! what sheaves to gather! 'A part have crossed the flood; a part are crossing now.' Here let your hearts revert with me to his own touching hymn, sung just now:

> *When my final farewell to the world I have said,*
> *And gladly lie down to my rest;*
> *When softly the watchers shall say, "He is dead,"*
> *And fold my pale hands o'er my breast;*
>
> *And when, with my glorified vision at last,*
> *The walls of "that city" I see,*
> *Will any one then at the beautiful gate*
> *Be waiting and watching for me?'*

'Waiting and watching!' Does he ask, Shall anyone be waiting and watching for me? My friends, when on this evening one week ago, by time of Earth, it was was announced in the courts of Heaven that this soldier of the Cross was about to be called to his reward; that the Lord's joy was full; that the crown was ready; and when the bright-liveried escort past the portals, what, think you, was there waiting and watching for him? Where was that glorious company—the seals of his ministry; the redeemed thousands gone before! Where the angelic host, with whom there had been joy eleven thousand times in heaven over those sinners repentant? Where the choirs seraphic? Yea, where the King himself? I trow [believe] there was waiting and watching at the beautiful gate! Nor watched nor waited long! From the smoking wreck of instant death, in the land of pain and sorrow, the released spirit shot upward, borne on wings swifter than the swift-winged light, it passed within the door opened in Heaven. Strain, strain the spirit's eyes to catch a glimpse of that welcome. The glittering throng; the sainted loved ones; his own eager thousands of the redeemed; the glad angels; the Master's plaudit; his Lord's joy; the everlasting crown; the stars that are to shine forever and ever! Son, daughter, of this sorrowing vale, let him 'rest' inside those beautiful gates of which he sang in such uncommon strains; within the walls of that city which, with glorified vision, he so longed to see! 'Well done, good and faithful servant, enter thou into the glory of thy Lord.'*

We leave him there. And now to you who loved him who loved you, and yet loves you: would you honor the man as is given man most to honor the dead? Then, in your minds and hearts, continue to hear the voice that is still. Remember his words; walk in his ways.

In the market-place of a German town there stands a statue, placed there by pious hands, of beautiful significance. High up over the bustling throng, where the people are buying and selling, and cumbered with the things of earth, there is a figure of an angel pointing heavenward, with a scroll in his hand, on which are these solemn words:

> *'Things that are seen are temporal;*
> *But the things that are not seen are eternal.'*

Could you adopt a truer, a more deserved reminder of the one that is gone, than, in sacred fancy, to behold him behind that vacant desk, where the memory will keep him long, pointing you ever, like the angel monitor of the busy mart, heavenward, heavenward! while from his unmoving hand you read his faithful teaching as you read God's warning:

> *'Things that are seen are temporal;*
> *But the things that are not seen are eternal.'*

Mr. Ross Tabb said:

*We have assembled tonight for the purpose of giving expression to our love for, and regret at, the loss of one who was with us, and of us, and now is not. Death has suddenly laid its hand upon our leader, and filled our order with mourning. A week ago this night a happy household expectant watched his coming; a few short hours past, and most unwelcome news—*DEAD*—crushes into the hearts of family and friends, and bows them down in very weakness. Never was a community more heavily shocked than by the announcement, 'Knowles Shaw is dead!' The short life he had spent with us had so interwoven itself with ours, that his death was our personal loss.*

But we bow in humble submission to this, to us, most terrible decree of our Father; sorrowing that he should call our beloved brother, in the very midst of his usefulness, from our people. Why it is that, in God's economy, such a man—whose life had been one untiring effort for the enlightenment and elevation of his fellows—should be given to the sickle of death, is beyond the ken of mortals; but we can only accept the fact, and say:

> *Judge not the Lord by feeble sense,*
> *But trust him for his grace—*
> *Behind a frowning Providence*
> *He hides a smiling face.'*

But, though our brother has gone from us, he yet speaks to his well-nigh broken-hearted people; bidding them to weep not, grieve not, falter not, but look forward to that beautiful, pure life promised in the hereafter to the faithful. The good that men do lives after them. Think you, my friends, the memory of such a man can perish? Will not his spirit dwell among us until the last pulsation of the heart cease? Will not the recollection of his kindnesses, his willingness at all times to relieve suffering, his steady rebuke of wrong in every guise, be an incentive to this people to occupy a higher plane of virtue and morality and Christian fellowship? Prominent actors in life's history live not to, nor for, themselves; and whether for good or evil, generations to come are shaped by their lives; if this be true, surely the world is the better for Knowles Shaw's living.

Eighteen months ago, as a stranger, he visited us. He labored with the Christian Church for a few weeks; and, by his energy, practical piety, and devotion to the cause, awakened an interest not alone in the church but the whole community. Crowded houses waited on his preaching. His church was awakened from its lethargy, and so impressed were they with his usefulness that he was asked to become their pastor. He cast his lot with us; and, from that time forward, his life was one of unceasing activity in all that tended to the moral and spiritual advancement of this people; and he lived the song he loved so well: 'Scatter seeds of kindness for the reaping by and by.'

He became interested in the question of Temperance; and, infusing his life into it, soon had the community aroused. He delivered powerful addresses in advocacy of the cause; and, as the result, over eighteen hundred persons, in this vicinity, joined the movement. He possessed, in a remarkable degree, the vitalizing power that made alive all with whom he was associated; with his convictions, life was too short to be wasted in fruitless efforts. He realized to a greater extent, than any one I ever knew—

> *A charge to keep I have,*
> *A God to glorify;*
> *A never-dying soul to save,*
> *And fit it for the sky.*

And with this high purpose in view, he labored faithfully to the end. His last work was a fitting crown to his life's labors. But he has gone from us. No more will we see him in this house, laboring with this church in the cause of Christianity, nor with this people in the work of Temperance.

We now have but the light of his example to beacon us on, but that light is full-orbed; and in fancy we can see him clothed in the garments of immortality, keeping guard over this people he loved so well. We know his wishes and zealous work in the cause of Temperance, and his untimely death should be an incentive to earnest work upon our part. Living as he lived, death had no terrors. He fully realized that ''twas not the whole of life to live, nor all of death to die;' and he left us the full exemplification of the beautiful lines:

> *So live that the summons comes to join*
> *The innumerable caravan that moves*
> *To the mysterious realms, where each shall take*
> *His chamber in the silent halls of death.*
> *Thou go not like the quarry slave at night,*
> *Scourged to his dungeon, but sustained and soothed*
> *By an unfaltering trust, approach thy grave*
> *Like one who wraps the drapery of his couch*
> *About him and lies down to pleasant dreams.*

Closing the exercises, the Rev. Dr. Lipscomb, of the Methodist Episcopal Church, said;

Mr. President, Ladies and Gentlemen:

I hesitate whether to attempt to draw the tribute I may offer, from the impressions which the life and character of Elder Knowles Shaw have made upon my intellect, or from those which personal intercourse and warm friendship have made upon my heart.

It is easy to estimate the character of most men. Strong, well-developed traits of intellect, or extraordinary physical endowments, command our admiration, while a luxuriant growth of the affections find an easy passage-way to our hearts. The one we can admire, but may not love; the other we can love, but may not admire.

Knowles Shaw could not be measured by either of these rules. He stands before us, in the combination of his nature and acquirements, one of the most peculiar men of the age. He might justly be called a human paradox—a natural anomaly.

His physical appearance was almost outre in its unusual peculiarities. Six feet three inches high; square and angular at every joint; long-armed, and long-limbed, he was straight as an American aborigine, and as muscular and active as a trained athlete. His eye was sharp and clear, and looked right before him, and his whole bearing was one of fearless aggression and personal prowess.

His huge hand seemed made to grasp a double-edged sword, as it cut down every opposing enemy. His huge foot was rightly placed when it crushed the necks of his foes. 'Forward' was written all over his physical being, and real strength backed every letter of the enstampment.

His mind partook largely of the peculiarities of his body. Self-educated, he had not learned to conform to the habits of the academy, nor was his brain illuminated by the lamp of the student. He learned as he lived, in the great world around him, and acquired knowledge as he needed it. He had no use for knowledge but to use it, and he used none but what was useful. His strong mind grasped truth vigorously, and he handled it with confidence and with power. Too direct for sophistry, too honest for claptrap, he spoke to the point, and drove his arrows to the mark. Aggressive, fearless, powerful, he stood the impersonation of an invading conqueror, before whom opposition must yield and every resistance withdraw.

In this world of ours the logical pathway of such a character would be written in blood, and enemies would everywhere spring up to dispute his progress. Hard blows are ever received upon an uplifted arm, and human hearts are wooed, not conquered. But, strange to say, Knowles Shaw had no enemies. The women loved him, the children loved him, the men loved him. Hearts opened to him as roses to the sunshine. Tears were the oftenest jewels he received, and human affection almost hedged up his moving footstep. Thousands flocked to hear him speak, thousands received his enunciations without reluctance or dissent. His sermons and speeches were oracular to his hearers, and current coin in immense territories of mind. Intellectual submission was co-extensive with the field of his labor, and his voice was the herald of his own success.

These things are the strange things that disturb our minds. Such success makes sad havoc with our established theories, and Knowles Shaw is still before us an enigma—a great human paradox. God is wonderfully wise; nature is wonderfully kind. There exists a great law, called by philosophers the law of compensation, that has a domain as wide as humanity, and opens into every department of man's nature. It fills vacuums with air, it puts flesh on bones, it lays smooth tracks over rough places, supplies deficiencies with excess, and makes power work as the handmaid of weakness. God knew Knowles Shaw in physique and brain was a merciless tyrant, and he placed within him that which would moderate the strength of his arm and soften the violence of his spirit. He gave him a great human heart, that filled every crook and cranny of his organism, that ran out to the extreme end of his longest finger, and pulsated in every foot-fall of his huge limbs. It saturated his very being with the love of his fellows, opened all his vision toward the woes and wants of men, and sent him an evangelist proclaiming 'good news' to the lost millions of earth—a herald of salvation and a soldier of the cross. It gave a melody to his voice that sent up to heaven magic wreaths of song, or wrapped his listening hearers in benedictions of joy. His tongue was tuned like an angel's harp, and its softest, sweetest notes were messages of consolation and words of hope to the weary and forlorn.

Did you ever hear him sing? Oh! the wonder that such a man was so mystically endowed. It was not the voice of a woman, nor yet of an angel; it was the voice of a MAN that had in it a ring half heaven, half earth— strong but sweet, magical but true. It could sing of Jesus and of sin; it could sing away the darkness and then rise on the strongest pinions of light; it could 'shiver' in the cold despair of the broken heart, 'drift away' into the loneliness of lost affection, and come back again bright as the face of a reformed drunkard's wife, and warm as the love of the happy children that clustered at her knee. God sent him out a singing evangelist, a hero with his harp, a warrior whose eyes sparkled with tears, and whose blows were for the healing of the nations.

His great heart destroyed his selfishness. He never worked for himself, he never fought for himself. He wanted no pelf in his pocket, nor bays on his brow. He worked and labored and fought for his Master and his brother. If he was strong, he used his power to lift up his fallen fellow-man. He struck for us, not against us. If he was brave, he used his courage to destroy our enemies, not us; and ten thousand dark fortresses of hell have felt his prowess as he rescued therefrom the poor fallen sin-stricken sons of Adam. His trophies are in this house, but he baptized them in his Master's name. Rescued ones are all around us, but we pay no ransom but love, and his highest joy was to point us to still higher heights, and help us on to where all is peace and safety forevermore.

The people of Columbus needed Knowles Shaw. I needed him. God sent him; and may your life and my life, stamped in the image of the Jesus he preached and the temperance he proclaimed, be to him the tribute we pay and the monument we rear.

None but men who felt what they said could give utterance to such sentiments as the above; and they serve to show how deeply Brother Shaw had impressed a community into which he had come less than two years before a stranger. While all the addresses were overflowing with true and deep feeling, I am sure that the reader will agree with me in regard to the last, that as a true, tender, and affectionate tribute to departed worth, it has seldom been equaled.

Chapter Eighteen

A Sad Scene—Strange Coincidence—Lines by G.W. Archer— Tribute of Affection—Memorial Service at Jackson, Mississippi—In Memoriam.

Sorrow for the sad fate of this faithful Christian soldier was mingled with deep sympathy for his stricken family. These kindred feelings found expression in a variety of ways, of which we give a few examples.

The following we take from the Columbus, Mississippi, papers:

REV. KNOWLES SHAW.

The melancholy fate of this great and good man has saddened our entire community. Singular that he and his friend and fellow-laborer, Bliss, should both have been the victims of a railroad disaster. The last sermon he preached before leaving us for Texas had much with regard to what he wanted his people to do in case he never returned to them. Without expressing any premonition of his fate, he counseled them as though he was stepping into eternity. An army of good deeds are trooping up to heaven to bear testimony to his zeal, his fidelity, and exemplary Christianity. The world, and not Knowles Shaw, is the loser by this railroad disaster.

***

One of the saddest scenes we ever witnessed was at the residence of the late Elder Knowles Shaw on Sunday night. By request of the family, the ministration of the Lord's Supper was held there instead of at the church. Dr. Curtis delivered a discourse upon the philosophy of death, with a beautiful tribute to the honored dead. Dr. Lipscomb offered up a pathetic prayer for the consolation of the living. There were other sympathizing friends from the various churches, and it was a commingling of Christian faith and sorrow we never want to see again.

The bereft household, consisting of father-in-law, wife, daughter and son, together with Miss Leonora Norris, left on the train for Rushville, Indiana, the next morning—'sorrowing most of all that they should see his face no more.'

The following incident is noteworthy:

It is a coincidence not a little singular, that on the afternoon of the day of his death, a drunken fellow in Columbus, Mississippi, mounted a box in a saloon and announced that he would 'preach Knowles Shaw's funeral.' He then proceeded to abuse him for his war upon the whisky traffic, and while speaking was attacked with an epileptic fit, from which he did not recover for hours. In the meantime the dispatch from Dallas was received in Columbus, announcing the fatal accident. It had not been known before, and the circumstance created no little excitement.

The lines which follow are by G.W. Archer, of Baldwyn, Mississippi:

*Soldier, unclasp thy trusty sword
and lay thy shield aside;
For the Master thou hast nobly fought
and for the Master died.*

*Earnest zeal and constant toil
thy unfaltering faith attest;
And He who heard thy earnest wish
has called thee home to rest.*

*Thy work was grand indeed!
and great indeed thy loss!
For now no more thy clarion voice
shall 'rally to the cross.'*

*Thy powers of speech and song
a tender chord could thrill,
But now, alas! the song is hushed,
the powerful voice is still!*

Thousands have felt thy power
and heard thy warning call
Who live today to bless thy name
and mourn thy sudden fall.

Hundreds have listened to thy strains,
and still with wonder heard,
Who bowed their heads in humble trust
obedient to the Word.

Soldier, go sing the victor's song,
receive the conqueror's crown,
For thou wast faithful to thy trust
and at thy post was found.

Go sing that 'wondrous new made song,'
where saints and angels dwell,
And those that thou hast turned from sin
will soon its chorus swell.

No notice better deserves to be called a "tribute of affection " than this:

One of the most useful and honored men that ever blessed this or any other community with his presence and example has been suddenly, and, without warning, hurled into eternity. Elder Knowles Shaw, the 'Singing Evangelist,' and pastor of the Christian Church at this place, was killed by a railroad accident near Dallas, Texas, on the 7th instant, while on his return home from a preaching tour of five or six weeks to that city.

Of course we have neither the capacity, the facts in hand, nor yet the heart to do any thing even approaching the shadow of justice to the life, labors, or talents, of such a man as Knowles Shaw. Looking to the standard journals of his church to perform that important task, all we can do here is to scatter a few flowers of love upon his grave, and mingle our tears with those of the thousands over the land who have listened to his marvelous eloquence and felt the magnetism of his godly example.

Mr. Shaw was born, as we have understood, in the State of

Indiana, and when killed had attained about his forty-fifth year. Born of poor parents, and deprived early in life of his father, for many years his existence was one long struggle with ill-fortune; but by indomitable pluck, integrity, and native genius, he conquered an education, helped his widowed mother, and became one of the brightest lights in the pulpit of the 'Church of the Disciples.' As he attained to years of early manhood he entered somewhat into the dissipations of youth, but becoming convinced of the value of a Christian's life, he put aside his violin and gave up the ball-room, and henceforth his career became one of glorious results in the spread of the gospel. For eighteen or twenty years his fame has been all over the North, among the people of his faith, as an evangelist of unequaled powers, and as a 'sweet singer in Israel,' that ranked him with the gentle and pious P.P. Bliss, of equally mournful memory. It was Mr. Shaw's habit to keep a diary of his evangelical labors. At one time during the year 1877, he showed the writer the last entry of the persons baptized by his own hands in the seventeen years of his ministry. They footed up the marvelous number of over eleven thousand! To a minister of ordinary physical powers, zeal, or stationary life, the above figures would seem incredible—nay, they would be impossible—but it must be remembered that Elder Shaw was peculiarly an evangelist. His musical gifts, both vocal and instrumental, were wonderful; his energy and zeal in the cause of truth were amazing, and his powers of physical endurance such as are not possessed by one man in ten thousand. These, added to the spotless purity of his private life, and his dauntless presentation of the truth everywhere and on all occasions, make it easy enough to understand how one man could accomplish such a work in such a comparatively brief period of time.

It seems that Rushville, Indiana, was most entitled to be called his old homestead, and thither his mourning family have followed the remains to their final resting- place. Before coming to Columbus, upon the call of this congregation, he preached two years in the city of Chicago, while the grand scope of his labors extend from Pennsylvania, in the East, to Kansas in the West. In the field of spiritual song he had published five books, and had nearly ready for the press when he died a volume of sermons.

But what are all these, and many other outside facts, in comparison with the knowledge of Brother Shaw that all of us here in Columbus have of him, and keep in such precious remembrance! About a year and a half ago he came to this city and began a series of discourses in the church. It was at the time of the 'big snow.' Since then (and we know we shall not be accused of denominational partiality in the statement) he has retained a hold upon the intellectual, the religious, and the social attention of the community, that has never found a parallel in her midst. Even those who differed from him most upon points of doctrine never for a moment doubted the resistless sincerity of his convictions, while how like moral cowards do we all feel and seem in contrast with that heroic courage that never hesitated to tell the truth upon any subject, and upon all occasions!

But the great, the starry beauty of his character, was its noble consistency. Just what he appeared in the pulpit and on the streets, he was indeed at home, or in the social circle—always impetuous, busy, kind, charitable, and affectionate. If he was oftentimes harsh in his form of expression, no man was more ready to make amends; and while he never would compromise what he felt to be the truth, he always said he never intended to wound. Only toward the Devil and his works could it be said he bore ill-will. His private life abounded with words and deeds of charity. It may literally be said that 'he went about doing good,' and this to a degree explains the fact that he was ever a poor man in this world's goods.

Perhaps nothing but his terrible death would have recalled the fact that of late months Brother Shaw has more than once expressed, in his own touching language, 'a longing for rest.' He had overtaxed his powers and knew it, and having accomplished great good, he perhaps felt that he deserved temporary relief from his labors. In his farewell sermon, before going upon his last trip, he seemed to have a presentiment of his fate—at least he alluded to the fact that we might never see each other again, and he wanted us to pray for him, and if we were not permitted to meet again on earth, we could all see each other in heaven. Nothing the writer ever heard could exceed the pathos and tenderness of that sermon; and so heart-aching is the memory of it now that, coupled with a mournful realization, almost makes us wish we had never heard it. If a parting under special divine guidance could ever suggest a scene of today, surely we commit (we know we intend) no sacrilege in likening it to that of Paul and his sorrowing disciples on the eve of the apostle's final departure to Jerusalem.

And now it seems strange that we who knew and loved him so well shall never be permitted to look upon his face again. That the giant form, the hearty salute, the bright, beaming eye, the awkward grace, the warm grasp of hand, the glorious voice, the melting tongue (the tongue so full of heart and the Savior's love one almost forgot the power of logic that upheld it), are all lost and hushed in the thrall of death. Only sweet and tender memories—only an example jeweled with countless deeds of Christian faith and practice — remain to us, pointing to a higher sphere, where all partings are unknown, where no tears are shed, 'where the wicked cease from troubling, and the weary are at rest!' May God help us all, for Christ's sake.

J.A.S.

Columbus, Mississippi, June 10, 1878.

The impression made in scores of public places may be learned from the next extract, taken from the *Christian Standard:*

MEMORIAL SERVICE.

A TRIBUTE FROM THE CHRISTIAN CHURCH, THE TEMPERANCE PEOPLE, AND THE COMMUNITY OF JACKSON, MISSISSIPPI, TO THE MEMORY OF ELDER KNOWLES SHAW.

Sunday evening, August 4, 1878, a memorial service was held in the Christian Chapel, in this city, commemorative of the life and services of the late Elder Knowles Shaw.

The meeting was opened in due form, and its object announced by the pastor, when Dr. S.R. Jones was called to the chair, and J.C. Johnston appointed secretary.

Col. F.T. Cooper then offered the following resolutions, which, after discussion, in which F.T. Cooper, J.W. Harris, H. Musgrove, and J.L. Power, took part, were unanimously adopted:

PREAMBLE.

On the 7th of June, 1878, Elder Knowles Shaw was killed in a railroad wreck in Texas, between Dallas and McKinney, after having just concluded a successful series of Christian meetings at the former place. A few moments previous to this disaster he was conversing with a Methodist preacher, and the last words which fell from his lips upon mortal ears were, 'Oh! it is a grand thing to rally the people to the Cross of Christ!' With these inspiring words ringing upon the air, the crash came which suddenly and tragically transferred him to another sphere. They are words of great import. They speak a sentiment of heavenly sublimity, and give a just clue to the character of the man. Perhaps it was a fitting finale to a life of purity and devotion, of continued success, and without a reproach, that he should quickly be brought face to face with his Master with these talismanic words fresh upon his mouth.

Only a few short weeks ago Elder Shaw labored in this church for the cause of Christ, temperance, and humanity. His zeal, his eloquence, his magnetism, have left their impress upon the hearts of our people of all classes. We remember him as the earnest and faithful Christian evangelist, as the fearless champion of the truth, as the untiring friend and laborer in the promotion of temperance, as the devout and consecrated man of God, whose soul went out in sweet charity and benevolence to the whole human race, and whose indomitable will never flagged in good works. His untimely death has spread a gloom over us, and we, as temperance people, as members of his church, as friends of the gospel, as an entire community, desire to testify our appreciation of his worth, our keen sense of bereavement at his death, and to give formal expression to the sorrow that fills our hearts. Therefore, we declare:

Resolutions.

1. That although in the death of Elder Shaw, his church, the temperance people, and the Christian world, have felt the giving way of one of their stanchest pillars of strength, and we have lost a friend whom we had learned to love and honor, yet we will not murmur at the rulings of Providence. We recognize his death as a great loss to us and the holy cause he so unwaveringly plead, but at the same time we recognize it as a great gain to him. Hence we invoke the consolation of that sublime Christian submission found in the language of our Redeemer, 'Father, thy will be done!'

2. That we cordially approve of and will cheerfully cooperate with the Knowles Shaw Monument Association of Rushville, Indiana, and consider it a privilege to contribute our mite to the erection of a suitable monument to the dead evangelist, and for the support of his surviving family.

3. That we tenderly express our condolence to the grief-stricken widow and orphans of our deceased brother, and while we would not insult their agony by comparing our feelings and sufferings with theirs, yet we hope to temper the heavy calamity to them as much as we can by the assurance of a heartfelt and sorrowful sympathy.

S.R. Jones, Chairman.

J.C. JOHNSTON, Secretary

MR. COOPER'S SPEECH.

Mr. President:—In presenting these resolutions for the action of this memorial meeting, I desire to add a word or two of comment. To many persons it may appear strange that I should appear in this role, and evince so much genuine feeling toward the memory of a man with whom I was scarcely acquainted personally. I never saw him until he held his meetings here in this chapel a few months ago. I am not a member of his church—alas! perhaps I am not fit to be a member of any church—but I attended several of his meetings here, and confess that I was impressed by him as I have been impressed by few men, with a profound respect and honor for the man. I saw in all his movements, heard in all his utterances, read in all his gestures, and realized in all his songs, the evidences of a sublime devotion, and a singleness of purpose, looking to the salvation of souls and the amelioration of his fellow- men. His face was aglow with enthusiasm. There was fire in his eye, resolution in his bearing, earnestness in his speech, and eloquence in his song. 'Oh, brethren,' he would often exclaim, 'let us sing eloquently.' And he did sing eloquently. It was here in this house, and under his voice, that I first fully realized the power and the true eloquence of song.

Is it strange that such a man should inspire homage in my bosom? The interest which he then awakened prompted me to watch his movements since, and to read snatches of his history in the various newspapers of the country. I learn from these sources of information, that although Elder Shaw was comparatively a young man, and suddenly translated from earth to heaven in the meridian of his life and at the zenith of his fame, yet he has baptized with his own hands about twelve thousand persons.

What a work is this? How shall we measure its greatness? A grand moral army rallied to the cross!

I would not exaggerate the magnificent results of the active life, but here are twelve thousand personal witnesses to magnify and praise them—twelve thousand gladdened souls who have drank the waters of life administered by his individual hands. And when we come to consider the vast crowds that have flocked to his revivals, and afterward sought comfort in other churches, and the solemn rite of baptism from other hands, it is impossible to tell— it is a thing known only to infinite intelligence—how many thousands of souls have been quickened under the magic of his ministration!

I learn also, from these same sources, that this man, Elder Shaw, began his evangelical work early in life, and that for the last fifteen or twenty years he has been 'going about doing good,' with no thought of self, absorbed, intensely absorbed in his mission, apparently as free from the allurements of the flesh and the sordidness of avarice as the apostles of old. At, last he fell, translated in a twinkling, in the full vigor of health, manhood, and intellect, at the prime of life, in the midst of his expanding and ripening field of usefulness, without a moment's warning, he was tragically cut off—but, like all true soldiers desire to fall, if fall they must, he fell with his full armor on—'he fell at his post.'

He has left a record of wonderful activity, and without a flaw. His success has been marvelous, and there is no taint upon it to mar its sweetness. The man does not live who can rise up now and point to a single blot upon his escutcheon. Surely such a character—so nearly perfect, so true, so devoted, so free from all the corroding cankers of humanity—deserves homage. In commemorating his virtues, we exalt our own natures. In honoring him, we honor ourselves."

We close this chapter with the following verses by Miss Mollie McGee, of Columbus, Mississippi, which were read at the memorial service, of which we have already given an account:

IN MEMORIAM.

***We** are journeying in the shade,*
***He** where flowers never fade.*
***We** are in the gloom of night,*
***He** where pinions flash with light.*
***We** are weary, tempest tossed,*
***He** where rest is never lost.*

*We **'neath** Heaven's mighty dome,*
*He **within** that sacred home.*

We with hearts with grief now riven,
He with brow now crowned in Heaven.
We with songs that soonest tire,
He with glad angelic choir.
*We **from** lost ones stand apart,*
*He **with** lost ones heart to heart.*
We yet to cross Death's icy river,
He by Life's Fount to live forever.

We with earth's pilgrims in the dust,
He with seraphim and the just.
*We to learn **still** more of sorrow,*
He to dread no coming morrow.
We with steps that go astray,
He safe beyond life's rugged way.
We on earth with blinded eyes,
He lives with God in Paradise!"

Chapter Nineteen

Poem—What the "Christian" and "Standard" Said—Challen's Last Song—Farewell.

The loving and tender words found in the preceding chapters seem doubly so when it is taken into account that some of the speakers and writers were of different religious denominations, but who, by intercourse with Brother Shaw, had learned to know and love him. His own brethren, all over the land, paid fitting tributes to his memory. Of these we can only give a few. With the sad news of his death there came a request that the author should embody his own sentiments and those of others in verse. This was done briefly as follows:

IN MEMORY OF KNOWLES SHAW.

*Gone in his prime—too soon, alas! too soon
For us the sudden, startling summons came,
Which called our brother from our sight away,
Swift as the prophet in his car of flame.*

*A precious gift of God he was to us;
To have him with us long we all were fain;
So dear he made himself to all our hearts,
We feel it hard to give him back again.*

*Sweet as the songs of Judah's shepherd king
To Israel, his songs to us shall be;
Sweeter, now that the singer sweet has gone,
And deeper graven on our memory.*

*A reaper in God's harvest, many sheaves
By his strong hand were safely gathered in;
And his shall be the bright reward of those
Who to God's service precious souls shall win.*

*A red cross knight, without reproach and fear,
Fresh from a battle nobly fought and Won;
Seeking another field he bravely fell,*

Just as he wished, with all his armor on.

His soul is now with Christ in paradise;
Why, then, should we, who loved him so, be sad,
When his freed spirit from its happy home
Looks down in love upon us, and is glad?

All the papers of the brotherhood of which Brother Shaw was a member, made fitting mention of his life and labors. We have only room for the two following—the first from the *Christian:*

BROTHER SHAW IS DEAD.

We know this announcement will carry sorrow for thousands of hearts as it has already to our own. The city papers of last Saturday contained a dispatch from Galveston, Texas, announcing a railroad accident one mile south of McKinney, on the Texas Central, in which thirteen persons were dangerously wounded and Brother Shaw killed. The accident was caused by a broken rail and rotten ties. The coach in which Brother Shaw was riding was precipitated down an embankment, forty feet, turning over three times, and stopping in two feet depth of water. Brother Shaw was under the car, and had to be cut out. A hole had been cut in his head, and he was dead when rescued from the car. Today (Monday) we are in receipt of the following card, which not only confirms the sad news of Brother Shaw's death, but gives Brother Baxter's name as one of the wounded:

McKinney, Texas, June 7, 1878.

Editors Christian:—Our beloved Brother Knowles Shaw is dead. He was killed in a railroad accident near this place this morning. He was coming to hold us a meeting. Had just closed a grand meeting at Dallas, with one hundred and twelve additions. Brother Baxter is badly hurt, but, we hope, not dangerously.

Your sister, ELLA M. PRICE.

Thus the sweet singer, the tender and tearful pleader with sinners, the great evangelist, the untiring and unceasing worker for Christ, has been cut off suddenly, in the prime of his life and in the midst of his usefulness. Over eleven thousand souls have been won to Christ by the gospel as sung and preached by him. Few men among us, if any, have so large a circle of personal acquaintances as Brother Shaw had. He has held meetings in many States of the Union, and in most of our principal cities. Thousands have thus learned to love him for his works' sake, and will mourn to learn of his violent death. Our own heart is too sad to say much now. At another time we hope to give our readers a suitable notice of the life and labors of this remarkable man of God.

Brother Shaw could not be regarded as a man of extraordinary intellectual grasp, or great logical power. He could make a plain argument, and was not without the power of correct reasoning; but his greatness did not consist in these things. His heart-power, and exhaustless enthusiasm, that seemed to flow like a perennial fountain; his accurate knowledge of, and deep sympathy with, humanity in its humblest conditions—these were his resources of power. The vilest sinner that ever came tremblingly forward to confess Christ, under his appeals, was met with the same glad welcome that he extended to those in the highest social position. To save sinners was, with him, a controlling passion. For this he lived and labored, and in pursuance of this grand work he died.

Few men have such power to reach the hearts of people as that possessed by our lamented evangelist. We have often seen whole congregations in tears, including hardened sinners, as he narrated, in his own inimitable way, some touching incident, usually connected with his own experience in the labor of the gospel. We have never heard a man so gifted in the power of exhorting his brethren and sisters to be faithful in their Christian duties. His day-talks to the members exceeded anything we have ever heard from any other man, taking them through a whole meeting.

We have often longed for his exhaustless flow of enthusiasm and hopefulness. Nothing damped his ardor. He began a meeting with the expectation that it was to be a glorious revival, and worked under the stimulus of that confident hope, without flagging in his zeal or good cheer. Gloomy weather, small audiences, and other kindred circumstances that cool the ardor of most men, had no such effect on him. He talked as well to a dozen hearers that had come out through a storm to hear him as to a crowded house. There were the same beaming face, tuneful voice and tearful eyes, pleading with sinners to be reconciled to God, and brethren to cling closer to Christ.

There are those who could not approve all his methods of work, and certainly some of them, if used by anybody else, would seem entirely out of place; but he was himself, and had his own way of working, and God blessed his work; and, while we may criticize his methods, few of us can be as efficient as he was in winning souls to Christ.

It is especially comforting to know, in this sad hour, that while his eccentricities and idiosyncrasies have sometimes been criticized, his fair name is unstained by even the breath of suspicion. His character as a Christian, in all his labors as a preacher of the gospel and as the author of several popular musical works, is, so far as we know, without reproach.

May God bless his bereaved family, whose hearts are crushed by this sad calamity, and the thousands of his converts who will be grieved by the news of his death. He has died like a soldier, on the field of duty, with his armor on. His spirit, like that of the lamented Bliss, took its departure from earth amid the terrible crash of a railroad disaster; thus emphasizing the lesson he has so often taught about the importance of being always ready. When we shall all of us, 'Gather round the great white throne,' among the voices of the innumerable choir that shall 'Sing God's praise through endless days,' we shall doubtless hear the swelling tones of our beloved evangelist, ascribing praise and honor and dominion to that Savior whom he loved so well and served so faithfully.

We pray for Brother Baxter's speedy recovery, lest we have sorrow upon sorrow.

We are indeed grateful to God that Brother Baxter was spared to his family and to the Church of God. And we are grateful, that, since Brother Shaw has been taken from us, he leaves so bright an example of earnest and heroic devotion to the Master. Fitting words are these with which to close such a life: 'Oh! it is a grand thing to rally people to the Cross of Christ!' May his brethren in the ministry catch the inspiration of these, his last words, and lift higher the banner of the cross, so that in his death, as well as in his life, he shall have given a renewed impetus to the cause he loved so well."

The *Christian Standard*, after giving the sad intelligence of his death, says:

It thus appears that suddenly, without a moment's warning, this earnest, ever-busy servant of God was called home. In death, as in life, there was dispatch. We judge that, if he had been consulted about the time and manner of his death, he would have said: 'Let it be when the Lord will, and let it be without long waiting, or lingering disease.' As one of our sweetest sacred poets has expressed it—

> *O that without a lingering groan*
> *I may the welcome call receive;*
> *My body with my charge lay down,*
> *And cease at once to work and live.'*

We made the acquaintance of Brother Shaw some eighteen years ago, when we accompanied Alexander Campbell on a preaching tour through Indiana. It was at Rushville. He was just beginning to feel his strength as a preacher. He was clear-headed, but with a tinge of enthusiasm in his work, and a ceaseless restlessness of manner, which foreshadowed the untiring energy with which he prosecuted his labors until his dying moment. In all seasons, in all places, under all circumstances, he was the same hopeful, earnest, indefatigable worker, whether in the pulpit or out of it. With ability to preach the gospel clearly, pointedly, fearlessly, he mingled some eccentricities of style, manner, and action, which excited curiosity, and sometimes subjected him to sharp criticism. But his manner was his own, and befitted him alone. Of his purity of life and singleness of purpose none that knew him entertained a doubt. His dear love of music, and his genius for poetical and musical composition, he made tributary to his one great passion—the salvation of souls. His success as a preacher was greater than that of most preachers—nor was he lacking in the qualities essential to a teacher. For incisive, pungent, fearless application of scripture doctrine he had few equals. His sudden departure, in the prime of life, at a time when he was achieving great success, can not but be mourned by myriads as a great loss to the church and to humanity. To his family, this sudden bereavement will be a crushing calamity. May the God of all consolation comfort their hearts in this season of bitter anguish. Let the living be animated and strengthened to greater zeal and devotion by the bright example of this remarkable man, and let us all be ready for the summons from the Master, for in such an hour as we think not, the Son of Man cometh.

As a fitting close of these notices, we can think of nothing better than the following spirited song, which was written by the venerable Elder James Challen, of precious memory, in his seventy-seventh year. It was the last production of his pen:

KNOWLES SHAW—THE DEAD EVANGELIST.

His last words before he was killed on a wrecked train of a railroad in Texas, June 7th, 1878, were, ''Tis a grand thing to rally the people to the Cross of Christ.'

'Twas the battle-cry of one who was coming from the field,
Who in courage never faltered, and to fear would never yield,
With his armor bright and perfect, and with ready sword in hand,
As he bore the cross of Jesus in triumph through the land.

Chorus,
'Tis a grand thing to rally the people to the cross,'
And for the name of Jesus to count all things but loss:
To lift on high his banner, who died our souls to save,
And faithful in his service, to be earnest, strong and brave.
Rally, rally, rally to the cross,
To the cross of Him who died a ruined world to save.

In the vigor of his youth, and with talents rich and rare,
With a faith that never faltered, and a soul to do and dare,
He gave his life to Jesus—Him who died for me and you—
And was faithful to his Leader, and to his conscience true.

Chorus.

He preached the cross of Jesus to sinners night and day,
And drew them to the Savior, the true and living way;
At home, in large assemblies, he taught both young and old,
And urged his fellow soldiers the ancient Fort to hold.

Chorus.

He sung the songs of Zion, with heart and lips afire;
With consecrated soul and voice he struck the trembling lyre;
With words of invitation, he melted, conquered, won;
Till his work of faith was finished, and his earthly race was run."

Chorus.

Numerous as are the extracts given, they form only a small part of what was said and written concerning him. From these, however, we cannot fail to gather the impression that was made in every community where he was known, by his life and labors. His whole life was one of great activity. He would not have died unknown, even if he had directed his energies into some other channel.

His religious life was one of entire consecration; he gave himself, with all his powers, to the Master's service. He entered upon that life with a noble purpose, pursued it with untiring effort, was eminently successful in winning souls—his converts numbering eleven thousand four hundred—nearly six hundred for every year of his ministry—and fitly ended his earnest, useful career, with the memorable words, which for years to come shall arouse a kindred spirit in others, "Oh! it is a grand thing to rally the people to the Cross of Christ." Then, till the dawning of the endless brighter day,

Farewell, dear brother, while our falling tears
But feebly tell how much we mourn thy loss,
May thy example lead us all, like thee,
To rally sinners to the Savior's cross.

www.ingramcontent.com/pod-product-compliance
Lightning Source LLC
Chambersburg PA
CBHW070549050426
42450CB00011B/2785